W9-BNP-056

EXPLORE THE BLACK HILLS, BADLANDS & DEVILS TOWER

Black Hills
Family Fun Guide

BY KINDRA GORDON

Adventure Publications, Inc.
Cambridge, Minnesota

DEDICATION

To my husband Bruce who I thank for helping me pursue my dreams.

Cover and book design by Jonathan Norberg

Photo credits by page number:

Cover photos: South Dakota Tourism: Pactola Reservoir (middle inset) and biking (right inset) **Kindra Gordon:** Flintstones Bedrock City (left inset) **Shutterstock:** Mount Rushmore (main photo)

Beautiful Rushmore Cave, Keystone, SD: 86 **Black Hills Badlands and Lakes Association:** 112 **Black Hills Central Railroad:** 103 **Borglum Historical Center:** 57 **City of Deadwood and the Deadwood Historic Preservation Commission:** 19 **Crazy Horse Memorial Foundation/Ace Crawford:** 9 (right), 17, **Crazy Horse Memorial Foundation/Robb DeWall:** 18 **Bonny Fleming:** 114 **Kindra Gordon:** 33 (right), 41, 43 (left), 46, 47, 76, 81, 111 **High Plains Western Heritage Center:** 53 **Homestake Visitor Center:** 43 **Paul Horsted:** 60 **Ken Jones/Fort Hays:** 120 **Brian Madetzke/Custer State Park:** 28 **The Mammoth Site of Hot Springs, SD:** 36 **Kathi Maxson:** 66 **National Presidential Wax Museum:** 14 **Randee Peterson:** 65 **Sioux Pottery:** 43 (right) 49 **South Dakota Tourism:** 8 (background), 9 (left, center), 16, 20, 22 (background), 23 (all), 26, 27, 29, 31, 32 (background), 33 (left, center), 38, 39, 40, 42 (background), 51, 52 (background), 53 (right, left), 56, 62, 63, 64, 68 (background), 69 (all), 72, 74, 75, 78, 79, 80, 82, 84, 85, 87, 90, 91, 92 (background), 93 (all), 96, 101, 105, 107 (both), 113, 116 (background), 117 (left) **Spirit of the Hills Wildlife Sanctuary:** 30 **Wall Drug Store, Inc.:** 106 (background), 110

10 9 8 7 6 5 4 3 2 1

Copyright 2007 by Kindra Gordon
Published by Adventure Publications, Inc.
820 Cleveland Street South
Cambridge, MN 55008
1-800-678-7006
www.adventurepublications.net
All rights reserved
Printed in China
ISBN-13: 978-1-59193-139-3
ISBN-10: 1-59193-139-8

2

INTRODUCTION

Wide open spaces, scenic vistas, gurgling streams—it's the stuff that dreams and cherished memories are made of, and you'll find it all in the Black Hills and Badlands of South Dakota.

Best known for the presidential faces of Mount Rushmore, this region often surprises visitors with its natural beauty, tranquil scenery and abundance of interesting places to explore. There's the monumental sculpture at Crazy Horse, and the natural grandeur of Devils Tower, Bear Butte, Spearfish Canyon, Custer State Park and the Badlands. You'll find one-of-a-kind museums, dinosaur displays and Broadway-style theaters. Add to this the excitement of tales of the Old West and narratives from Native American culture, and you've got more to experience than you can fit in just one family vacation!

The Black Hills offer adventure, history, family fun and even quiet solitude. It's a place people visit over and over again—for the granite spires, the black forest and the pleasant South Dakota pace. For families, it's a memorable destination that often becomes tradition from one generation to the next.

The *Black Hills Family Fun Guide* will complement your adventures and exploration of South Dakota's Black Hills and Badlands. Arranged by theme, this easy-to-read, fact-filled guide describes over 150 attractions— places to go and things to do—in this fascinating region. If you want to pose for an old-time photo, explore a gold mine, take a trail ride, or learn about the area's many patriotic places, this book provides the details of what's offered and where to go. Interspersed within the informative text are history, trivia and interesting tidbits to make your experience in the Black Hills meaningful. At the back of the book (page 130), you will find an index alphabetically arranged by city. So go ahead and explore, and most importantly, enjoy this fascinating region!

Neat to Know

➤ The Black Hills Visitor Information Center (east of Rapid City on I-90, Exit 61; 605-355-3700) is a helpful resource for planning any outing in the region. They offer brochures and maps for all Black Hills and Badlands destinations, restaurants, campgrounds and hotels. Another good resource is the Black Hills Badlands and Lakes Association of South Dakota website at www.blackhillsbadlands.com

Table of Contents

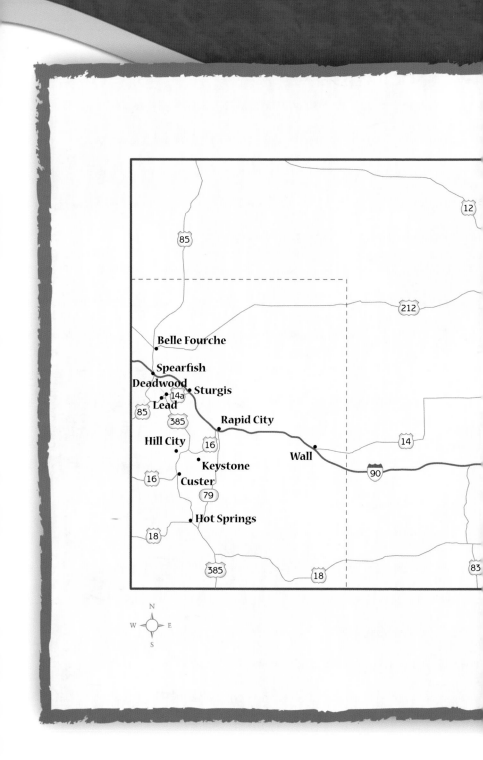

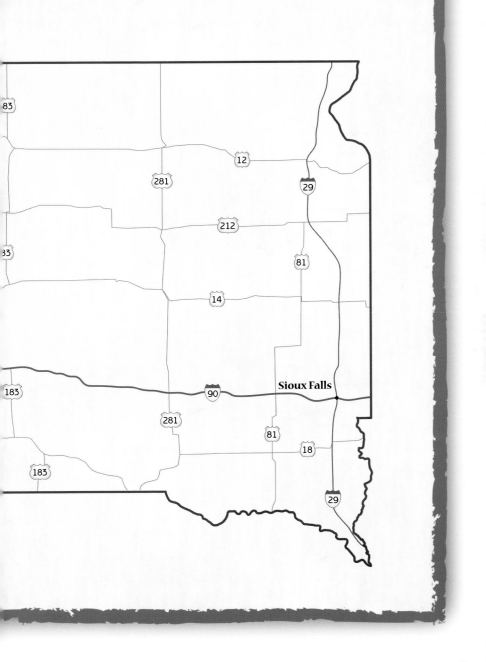

CHAPTER ONE

Famous Faces to Visit

Throughout the Black Hills are monumental tributes to famous people from the past. Of course, the titanic faces of Washington, Jefferson, Roosevelt and Lincoln carved in stone at Mount Rushmore is the most well-known memorial in this region, but there are many other Black Hills attractions that honor historical figures and share the stories of their lives. You'll find several sights with a presidential theme, as well as memorials to Native American leaders and Wild West legends.

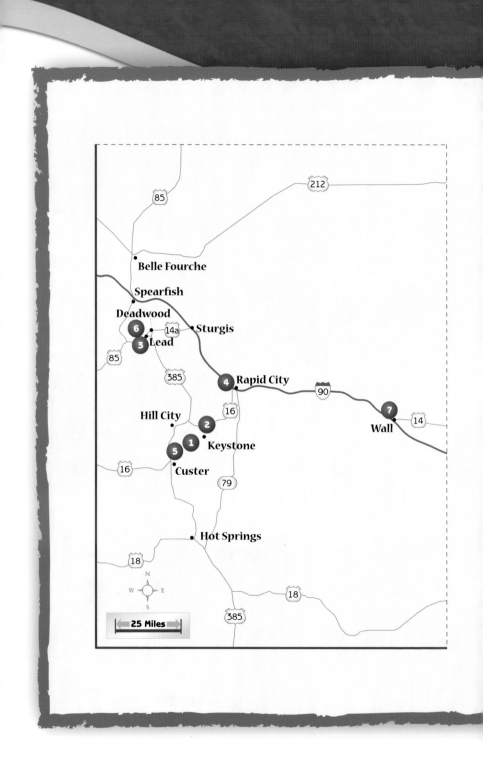

Presidential Places

Historical Figures

MOUNT RUSHMORE NATIONAL MEMORIAL

Carved from a mountain that stands more than a mile high, a visit to Mount Rushmore instills visitors young and old with a stirring sense of American pride. Created by sculptor Gutzon Borglum as a tribute to American ideals, the four presidents—George Washington, Thomas Jefferson, Abraham Lincoln and Theodore Roosevelt—were chosen to be part of the monument because they symbolized the birth, growth, preservation and development of the United States.

South Dakota's signature attraction is the presidential faces on Mount Rushmore.

In August 1927, Borglum began drilling on the mountain at the age of 60. After Borglum's death, his son Lincoln completed the project on October 31, 1941. It took a span of 14 years and cost nearly one million dollars ($989,992.32 to be exact) to carve the four faces, with $836,000 of that cost paid by the federal government.

Today, over three million people visit Mount Rushmore each year. Once you've admired the faces on the mountain, take time to explore and enjoy the grounds surrounding this symbol of our nation's democracy.

Fun activities include finding your home state's flag among the colorful **Avenue of Flags** that greets visitors as they enter Mount Rushmore. The promenade of flags leads to the **Grandview Terrace** for a majestic view of the Four Faces. Then, hike the paved **Presidential Trail** to get a close-up view of the granite sculpture. The trail makes a half-mile loop; the first quarter-mile of the path is wheelchair accessible. Mountain goats can often be spotted traversing the rock around Rushmore.

To learn more about the monument, watch the brief film at the **Lincoln Borglum Museum**, which explains how and why the monument was created. Then view the historical exhibits on display in the museum, including a mock dynamite blast for kids. Also plan to visit the **Sculptor's Studio** where Gutzon Borglum's original model of the monument and many of the tools used to carve the mountain are still kept.

A **Junior Ranger Program** is offered for children ages 5–12 that explains the carving of Mount Rushmore and teaches kids about the National Park Service. For children 13 and older (and adults) the **Rushmore Ranger Program** is designed to help develop an understanding and appreciation for national parks—with a special emphasis on Mount Rushmore. Each program includes a booklet for the individual to fill out. Ask about the programs at the Visitor Information Center near the entrance or call 605-574-3165 for more information.

The **Evening Lighting Ceremony** is an extremely popular Mount Rushmore event. This patriotic program in the outdoor amphitheater includes a short film about the monument and concludes as floodlights reveal the presidents' faces lit up against the night sky. From May through August the program is held at 9 pm nightly. In September, the program begins at 8 pm. From October through April, the sculpture is illuminated at dusk, but there is no program. Dress warm for the evening ceremony as night temperatures are chilly in the mountains.

Also at Mount Rushmore, be on the lookout for the white mountain goats that make their home in the jagged granite cliffs of the Black Hills. And be sure to drive around Mount Rushmore on State Hwy. 244 for a unique profile view of George Washington.

A bookstore, gift shop, restaurant and snack shop are also available on-site at Mount Rushmore National Memorial.

Open year-round; Admission is free, but a fee is charged for parking.
13000 Highway 244, Building 31, Suite 1, Keystone, SD 57751; 605-574-2523
www.nps.gov/moru

Neat to Know

➤ Western heroes such as Buffalo Bill Cody, Lewis and Clark and American Indian leaders were first considered for the monument.

➤ Jefferson's face was originally supposed to be on the left side of Washington's (as you look at the sculpture); it was moved to the right because of flaws in the rock.

THE NATIONAL PRESIDENTIAL WAX MUSEUM

Meet each of America's presidents as you walk through this unique museum. On display are realistic, life-size wax figures of every U.S. president in period costumes and historical settings, such as John F. Kennedy in the Oval Office with John Jr. playing beneath the desk, and Nixon aboard the U.S.S. Hornet welcoming the astronauts home from their moon flight. President Clinton's red, white and blue saxophone and Florida's controversial ballot boxes are among the intriguing exhibits at this museum.

A life-like wax display of John Jr. playing beneath JFK's desk in the Oval Office is one of the many exhibits at Keystone's Presidential Wax Museum.

Open April 1 to October 31; Admission charged.
Hwy. 16A, P.O. Box 238, Keystone, SD 57751; 605-666-4455
www.presidentialwaxmuseum.com

PRESIDENTS PARK

This 20-acre sculpture garden features larger-than-life stone busts of all of our nation's presidents. Each sculpture stands nearly 20 feet tall and was created by Texas sculptor David Adickes, who says he was inspired by the grandeur of Mount Rushmore, but wanted to create presidential monuments that were more approachable by visitors. The statues are arranged chronologically along a wooded trail of Ponderosa pines with informational displays providing biographical information about the president and his term in office. You may take a self-guided tour or arrange for a guided, themed tour, ranging in topics from Presidents in the military, assassination attempts and plots, or the First Ladies and their contributions. The park includes a gift shop and a snack bar.

You can get a sneak peak of three of these "heads of state" at the Presidents Park Information Center along Highway 16 between Rapid City and Keystone.

Open year-round; Admission charged. 11249 Presidents Park Loop, Lead, SD 57754; 605-584-9925 www.presidentspark.com

Sculptures of Ronald Reagan and all of the other U.S. presidents share history lessons at the Presidents Park near Lead.

Neat to Know

➤ Located near the scenic Mickelson Trail, which winds through the Black Hills, Presidents Park offers bicycle rentals on-site in the summer and fall and snowmobile rentals in the winter.

CITY OF PRESIDENTS PROJECT

Rapid City pays special homage to American history with life-size bronze statues of past U.S. presidents on downtown street corners. Crafted by South Dakota sculptors, each presidential sculpture is the actual height of that man and is dressed appropriately for the period in which he lived—Ronald Reagan in western attire, John Adams in a waistcoat and vest. The "City of Presidents" project began in 2000 and will add four bronze statues to the downtown area each year until all U.S. presidents are on display.

Look for the two Native American themed sculptures titled *Iye Na Oyate Ki* and *Mitakuye Oyasin* on display along Rapid City's Main Street as well.

Open year-round, Free admission. Information center at 631 Main St., Rapid City, SD 57709; 605-343-1744

Gerald Ford and Liberty, captured in bronze, stand among other presidential sculptures in downtown Rapid City.

Neat to Know

➤ Past presidents have found the Black Hills a favorite place to visit. In 1927, President Calvin Coolidge spent the summer at Custer State Park's Game Lodge and Resort earning it the nickname the "Summer White House." The resort was a favorite of President Eisenhower's too. (For more on Custer State Park, see Chapter 6, page 73)

Historical Figures

CRAZY HORSE MEMORIAL

This mountain sculpture of Lakota leader Chief Crazy Horse is being constructed as a tribute to North American Indians. Korczak Ziolkowski began carving Crazy Horse in 1948 at the request of Indian leaders who wanted to create a memorial that would complement Mount Rushmore and remind the world "that the Red Man has great heroes, too." Interestingly, Ziolkowski also worked on Mount Rushmore for a short time in 1939 with its creator Gutzon Borglum.

Despite Ziolkowski's death in 1982, his wife Ruth and seven of their ten children continue to work on the sculpture, which is a nonprofit project financed from private funds. In 1998, fifty years after the project was started, the nine-story-high face of Crazy Horse was completed. Blocking out the 22-story-high horse's head is currently in progress. Upon completion (which hinges on weather and financing), the figure of the great chief astride his pony will be 563 feet high and 641 feet long, the largest statue in the world.

Upon completion, the figure of Chief Crazy Horse astride his pony will be 563 feet high and 641 feet long, the largest statue in the world.

Although visitors can get a good view of the Crazy Horse Monument from Hwy. 385, the on-site **Orientation Center** provides an educational overview about the creation of the monument and of Native American culture. The informative film, *Dynamite and Dreams,* in the visitor center profiles Ziolkowski's vision for the Crazy Horse Monument and the surrounding campus. On-site displays include scale models of the statue and exhibits explaining the drilling and blasting process. Also on-site, the **Indian Museum of North America** features an extensive display of Indian artifacts such as beaded moccasins and an authentic tepee. The **studio-home and workshop** of Ziolkowski showcases sculptures he created through his lifetime. A bookstore, gift shop, restaurant and cultural center (where authentic Native American jewelry and art are offered for sale) are all located within the complex.

Blasting on the mountain occurs intermittently through the summer with a ceremonial blast held each October on Native American Day. The monument is lighted nightly at dusk for one hour. From Labor Day to Memorial Day a laser light show is held nightly at 9 pm. The show features colorful animations, still photography, sound effects and laser beams choreographed to music.

Open year-round; Admission charged.
Avenue of the Chiefs, Crazy Horse, SD 57730 (5 miles from Custer, SD);
605-673-4681
www.crazyhorsememorial.org

Thousands hike the mountain during the Annual Volksmarch at the Crazy Horse monument.

Neat to Know

➤ For visitor's who like to hike, the **Annual Volksmarch** (www.crazyhorse.org/events/volksmarch.shtml) is held the first full weekend in June and gives the public a once-a-year chance to hike up the mountain and stand in front of the nine-story-high face of Crazy Horse. Round-trip, the hike is 6⅓ miles.

➤ Crazy Horse was chosen for the mountain sculpture, even though there is no documented photo of him. It is said that he refused to have his photo taken, asking photographers, "Would you imprison my shadow too?" Thus, the sculpture of him is not a lineal likeness, but rather a tribute to the spirit of the man and is based on detailed descriptions of Crazy Horse.

MOUNT MORIAH CEMETERY

This hillside cemetery is the final resting place for many of the Old West's legendary characters. Most notable is Wild Bill Hickock, who was shot in Deadwood during a poker game on Aug. 2, 1876. A bronze monument marks his gravesite. Calamity Jane, who was born as Martha Canary and claimed to be Wild Bill's sweetheart, is buried beside him. Visitors to the cemetery will also see graves of Potato Creek Johnny, Preacher Smith, Seth Bullock (Deadwood's first sheriff) and others with historical ties to Deadwood. From Mount Moriah, visitors can get a bird's eye view of Deadwood in the gulch below.

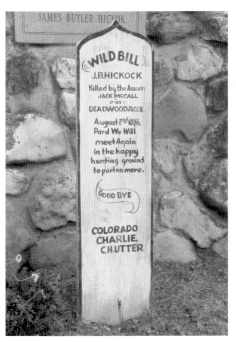

Wild Bill Hickock's tombstone.

To learn more about Deadwood's past, consider taking a narrated bus tour outlining the town's history and its colorful residents. Three bus companies offer similar one-hour tours that wind through Deadwood and stop at Mount Moriah. Tours are offered several times daily from May to October with pick-up points along Deadwood's Main Street. Tour companies include:

Original Deadwood Tours, 605-578-2091 or www.originaldeadwoodtour.com

Alkali Ike Tours, 605-578-3147 or www.deadwoodtours.com

Boot Hill Tours, 605-578-3758 or www.boothilltours.com

19

Old West history comes to life with the **Gunslingers Show**, a historical re-enactment of a Western shootout presented at 2, 4 and 6 pm daily along Deadwood's Main Street. These free street performances are given from Memorial Day through early September. For more information call 605-578-1876.

Enjoy the re-enactment of a Western shootout on Deadwood's Main Street.

A mock **Trial of Jack McCall** is another entertaining venue held nightly, Memorial Day through Labor Day in the Deadwood Theatre (the Masonic Temple next to the Silverado). McCall underhandedly shot the unsuspecting Wild Bill Hickock while Hickock was engrossed in a game of poker. His final hand was a pair of aces and eights, since known as the "dead man's hand." The re-enactment, which is held Sunday through Friday, begins at 7 pm inside Saloon No. 10 with actors portraying the poker game that led to the shooting. At 7:30 pm, the action moves to Main Street with the capture of McCall, and then the trial gets underway in the theater at 8 pm. The performance is historically accurate with a large dose of entertainment provided by audience participation. For information call 800-999-1876.

Open year-round; Admission charged.
Mount Moriah Road, Deadwood, SD 57754; 605-722-0837

Neat to Know: Deadwood History

➤ To this day, some say Seth Bullock haunts the **Bullock Hotel** (www.historicbullock.com) that he established in 1896 on Deadwood's Main Street. Thirty-minute ghost tours can be scheduled. For more information or for hotel reservations call the Bullock at 800-336-1876.

➤ **Saloon No. 10** at 657 Main Street, Deadwood, bills itself as a museum with antiques and oddities spread throughout the historical bar, including Wild Bill Hickock's death chair. Families are welcome to view the historical selection until 8 pm (605-578-3346 or 800-952-9398; www.saloon10.com). The original 1876 location of Saloon No. 10 was actually across the street at 622 Main Street, today known as the Eagle Bar at the Wild West Casino. When a fire claimed many of the buildings along that block in 1879, the bar moved up the street.

➤ Two famous women associated with Deadwood's Gold Rush lived in nearby Sturgis. **Annie Tallent**, the first white woman to come to the Black Hills in 1874, came to the area in search of gold. Her home at 1603 West Main Street is now a private residence. **Poker Alice**, a cigar-smoking card shark who owned the rowdiest honky-tonk in the state, also lived in Sturgis. Her home still stands at 1802 Junction Ave. Poker Alice is buried in St. Aloysius Catholic Cemetery, which is directly across from the Annie Tallent house.

➤ A great way to see Deadwood is to jump aboard the green trolleys that meander through town. The trolleys run at regular intervals between all hotels, motels and other key stops in Deadwood. Trolleys run year-round, and cost is minimal.

WILD WEST WAX MUSEUM

The stories of Wild West heroes such as **Jesse James**, **Wild Bill Hickock** and the movie star **John Wayne** are portrayed in the unique wax displays showcasing these legends. Over 25 figures in authentic Western costumes are on display.

Open mid-May through Labor Day, Admission charged.
601 Main Street, P.O. Box 441, Wall, SD 57790;
605-279-2915 or 605-279-2418

CHAPTER TWO

Buffalo, Bears and Reptiles, Oh My!

The Black Hills does not have a traditional zoo, per se, but it does offer many attractions with live animals on displays—from wildlife and reptiles to friendly farm pets. Options range from park-like settings where you can see animals up close to scenic drives through the region's state and national parks where wild animals roam free.

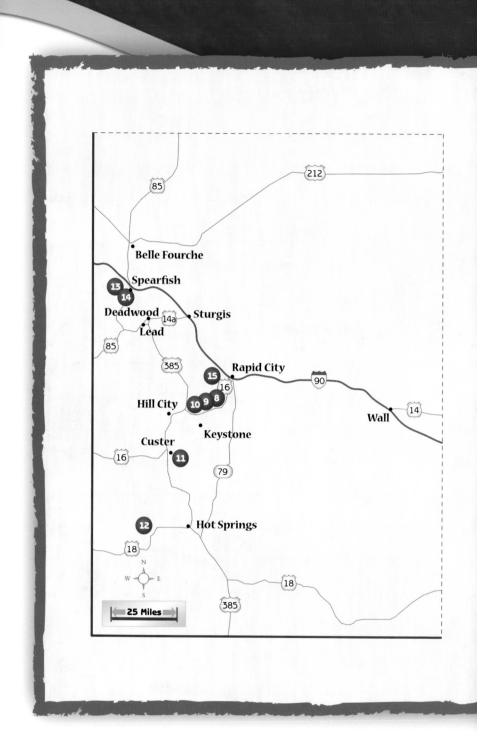

Animal Adventures

Fish Fun

REPTILE GARDENS

It goes without saying that most boys will love this place: snakes, komodo dragons, alligators, crocodiles and lizards are all here. But the rest of the family will be equally captivated by the many activities Reptile Gardens has to offer.

The educational show featuring alligators and crocodiles is thrilling for all ages.

Operating since 1937, Reptile Gardens is well-known for its extensive collection of reptiles, fossils and two big attractions (literally): Maniac, a 1,000-pound crocodile, and the giant tortoises that are over 100 years old. The Sky Dome is a jungle-like setting with free-flying birds and non-poisonous snakes moving amid tropical orchids and colorful, lush botanical plants. Four educational shows (Birds of Prey, Alligators and Crocodiles, Snakes and Bewitched Village) showcase the talents of trained animals and are presented several times daily during the summer months. Allow time to stroll the flower-filled grounds, visit the prairie dog exhibit (which includes an underground tunnel for kids and adults) and browse the reptile-themed gift shop.

Open April 1 to October 31; Admission charged.
P.O. Box 620 (6 miles south of Rapid City on Highway 16),
Rapid City, SD 57709; 605-342-5873 or 800-335-0275
www.reptile-gardens.com

BEAR COUNTRY U.S.A.

Visitors are guaranteed to see wildlife in this three-mile drive-through park that is home to black bears and grizzlies as well as bighorn sheep, reindeer, elk, Rocky Mountain goats and wolves. Opened in 1972, this privately owned collection of animals has grown to almost 300 black bears and other wildlife. Most of the animals are born on the premises and are hand-raised by the park staff. The Wildlife Center at the end of the park provides a walk-through area with exhibits featuring smaller wildlife in addition to baby bears, wolves and other young born in the spring. The Bear's Den gift shop and gallery caters to wildlife enthusiasts.

Open May 1 through October 31; Admission charged.
13820 South Highway 16 (8 miles south of Rapid City on Highway 16), Rapid City, SD 57701; 605-343-2290
www.bearcountryusa.com

Black bears are the main attraction at Bear Country U.S.A.

Neat to Know

➤ During the summer, Bear Country U.S.A. hosts several one-day "critter camp" sessions for kids ages 5–12. Participants will learn about the wildlife in the park and can enjoy games and arts and crafts. There is a fee for this animal adventure, which includes lunch, snacks, a t-shirt and a keepsake photo. For more information call 605-343-2290.

OLD MACDONALD'S PETTING FARM

Kids can get up close and personal with dozens of friendly farm animals at this petting zoo. Activities include feeding fish, ducks and geese in their ponds, bottle-feeding goats and calves, as well as pony and train rides. In the poultry house, you can even watch chicks hatch from their eggs. The whole family will have a squeal at the pig races (held five times throughout the day), and the goats trip-tropping over their very own bridge are always entertaining. There is a snack barn and gift shop on site, or pack a picnic and enjoy it at the play area. Guided tours, school field trips and special rates for birthday parties are available.

Open May 1 through Labor Day, then weekends only in September; Admission charged.
23691 Busted Five Court (9 miles south of Rapid City on Highway 16), Rapid City, SD 57702; 605-737-4815
www.oldmacsfarm.blackhills.com

CUSTER STATE PARK

At 70,000-plus acres, Custer State Park is truly the place where "buffalo roam and the deer and the antelope play." This well-known park, just south of Mount Rushmore, ranks as the nation's second-largest state park and is home to nearly 1,500 buffalo, along with elk, deer, bighorn sheep, prairie dogs and the "begging" burros (who aren't shy about approaching cars and begging for food).

Within the park, the 18-mile **Wildlife Loop** is a popular drive that often provides breathtaking views of the park's many animals. Several other scenic drives also wind through the park offering picture-perfect vantage points of forest, grassy valleys and abundant wildlife. **Needles Highway, Iron Mountain Road, Horse Thief Lake Road** and **Sylvan Lake Road** make up the 70-mile Peter Norbeck Scenic Byway, which has been named one of America's 10 Most Outstanding Byways.

Buffalo are always exciting to see in Custer State Park.

Of course you can do more than drive through the park. The **Peter Norbeck Visitor Center** on Hwy. 16A or the **Wildlife Station Visitor Center** on the Wildlife Loop are good starting points to learn more about the park and its activities, which include hiking, mountain biking, rock climbing, swimming, canoeing, paddle boating and trail rides. Visitors are also welcome to cross-country ski in the winter. The visitor centers can provide maps for trails in the park and information about the park's Junior Naturalist and Ranger Programs, which allow visitors to explore the outdoors and learn more about the Black Hills and Custer State Park.

For more activities available in Custer State Park, See Chapter 6, page 73

Open year-round, Admission charged.
HC 83, Box 70, Custer, SD 57730; 605-255-4515
www.custerstatepark.info

Neat to Know: Bevy of Buffalo

➤ Known for its large herd of buffalo, Custer State Park offers two unique opportunities to marvel at these shaggy beasts. Throughout the summer, **Buffalo Safari Jeep Rides** leave from the State Game Lodge in the park and allow visitors to get into the backcountry to see the buffalo roam. In the fall, Custer State Park conducts an **annual buffalo roundup**, allowing visitors to watch as the thundering herd of buffalo is moved into corrals where some animals will be sorted and sold in order to keep the herd a manageable size. For more information call 605-255-4515 or visit the website at www.custerstatepark.info.

BLACK HILLS WILD HORSE SANCTUARY

Wild horses run free on the open prairie of this 11,000-acre sanctuary. This working ranch was established by author and conservationist Dayton Hyde for the wild mustangs rescued from oversized herds on government lands in the West. Two-hour guided tours are offered several times daily and showcase these magnificent mustangs along the Cheyenne River wilderness that they now call home. Petroglyphs, tepee rings, the *Crazy Horse* movie set, abundant wildlife and a gift shop in a historical homestead farm building are highlights of the sanctuary. Portions of the 2003 Disney movie *Hidalgo* were also filmed at the Black Hills Wild Horse Sanctuary.

Wild mustangs roam free along the Cheyenne River wilderness south of Hot Springs.

Open April to October 31; Admission charged.
P.O. Box 998 (13 miles SW of Hot Springs on Hwy. 71), Hot Springs, SD 57747;
605-745-5955 or 800-252-6652
www.wildmustangs.com

Neat to Know

> ➤ On your way to or from the Wild Horse Sanctuary, plan a picnic stop at **Keith Park** or **Cascade Falls**, also found along Highway 71. Both spots offer scenic settings with natural flowing springs, picnic tables and restrooms. The cool waters of Cascade Falls are also considered one of South Dakota's best natural swimming holes.

SPIRIT OF THE HILLS WILDLIFE SANCTUARY

This working wildlife rehabilitation center has become a refuge for injured and orphaned domestic animals and wildlife, including exotic birds, lions and tigers. Educational tours are offered daily. Visitors can also take hayrides or hike in the Black Hills; in the winter, snowshoe, cross-county ski or enjoy a sleigh ride. The sanctuary is closed Mondays.

A special wildlife sanctuary near Spearfish provides refuge for a variety of animals.

Open year-round; Admission charged.
500 N. Tinton Rd., Spearfish, SD 57783; 605-642-2907
www.blackhills.com/bhpp/sh_index.htm

Fish Fun

D.C. BOOTH HISTORIC NATIONAL FISH HATCHERY

Established by the U.S. government in 1896, this hatchery played an instrumental role in introducing trout into the Black Hills and Yellowstone National Park. The U.S. Fish and Wildlife Service continues to use the facility to raise trout today. Buildings, including the elegant D.C. Booth House decorated in Victorian period furnishings, and the Hatchery Museum which features a railroad fish car, are open during the summer months. The scenic grounds are open year-round, and visitors can always feed the fish, ducks and geese in the ponds and get a nose-to-nose view of the large trout through underwater viewing windows.

Check out the trout through the underwater viewing windows.

Open year-round; Free admission.
423 Hatchery Circle, Spearfish, SD 57783; 605-642-7730
http://dcbooth.fws.gov/

CLEGHORN SPRINGS STATE FISH HATCHERY

This working hatchery raises and releases over 500,000 rainbow trout and Chinook salmon annually—primarily for stocking South Dakota's lakes and rivers for fishing. It's a popular place for field trips or family outings. The hatchery even provides free food to feed the fish. The hatchery's Aquatic Education Interpretive Center provides informative displays about fish hatchery operations, fly-fishing and stream rehabilitation efforts. From September through May, the hatchery accommodates scheduled tours Monday through Friday.

Open Memorial Day through mid-August; Free admission.
Hwy. 44 West, Rapid City, SD 57701; 605-394-4100
www.sdgfp.info/Wildlife/Fishing/Hatcheries/Cleghorn/CleghornIndex.htm

FOR MORE WILDLIFE SIGHTINGS, SEE ALSO:

Chapter 3: Badlands National Park, Wall, page 37

Chapter 6: Wind Cave National Park, Hot Springs, page 85

CHAPTER THREE

Dinosaurs Galore

Hundreds of dinosaur fossils have been uncovered across South Dakota, including the 1990 discovery near Faith, South Dakota of "Sue," the largest and most complete *Tyrannosaurus rex* ever found. While Sue is now on display at The Field Museum in Chicago, South Dakota's Black Hills still offer a variety of places where visitors can examine dinosaur bones and other prehistoric fossils and learn about the gigantic creatures that roamed the earth millions of years ago. Even younger children can get in on the dinosaur craze with light-hearted exhibits like Rapid City's Dinosaur Park and Custer's Flintstones Bedrock City.

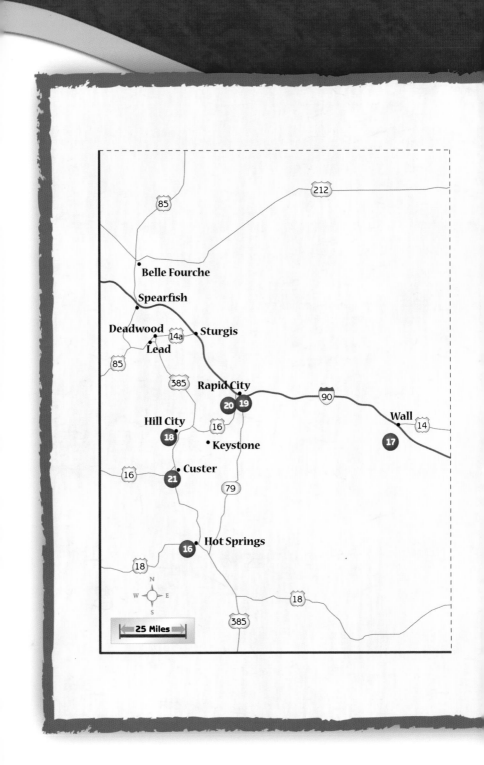

Fascinating Fossils

Dinosaur Delights

MAMMOTH SITE

The Black Hills' best-known fossil find is likely the Mammoth Site, an amazing prehistoric sinkhole where the fossils of over 100 mammoths (ancestors of the elephant) and other early creatures were perfectly preserved during the last Ice Age. The fossils, estimated to be about 26,000 years old, weren't discovered until 1974 when a bulldozer working on a housing project unearthed a mammoth tusk. The housing project was stopped and an enclosed research facility was eventually built over the fossilized sinkhole.

Researchers conduct actual fossil excavation every July at the Mammoth Site in Hot Springs, SD.

Today, visitors can take guided tours to view the actual excavation in progress. Walkways constructed over the site allow visitors to see the fossils as they are painstakingly unearthed. Active digs are only conducted in July, but tours of the site that show various stages of the excavation process are given year-round. More than 50 Columbian and woolly mammoths and other creatures from the Pleistocene era have already been excavated and about 50 more mammoths are still being dug out, making it the largest mammoth research facility in the world.

A museum adjacent to the excavation area includes displays of life-size mammoth replicas and features a mock dig area that lets kids excavate fiberglass fossil replicas. Youngsters ages 4 to 13 can even take part in the Junior Paleontologist Excavation, a simulated dig held daily from June 1 to August 15. (A small fee is charged for the hour-long session. Make reservations for the program by calling 605-745-6017.) Kids will also enjoy roaming the gift shop, which is stocked with prehistoric-themed books, puzzles, games and clothing.

Open year-round; Admission charged.
1800 Hwy18 By-Pass, P.O. Box 692, Hot Springs, SD 57747; 605-745-6017
www.mammothsite.com

BADLANDS NATIONAL PARK

Thirty-million-year-old fossils of three-toed horses, saber-toothed cats and giant rhinoceros-like beasts called titanotheres have been discovered among the rugged landscape of the Badlands. The **Ben Reifel Visitor Center** and the **Fossil Exhibit Trail** in this national park offer interpretive displays and fossil replicas that tell the story of these early Badlands creatures. The Visitor Center includes natural history exhibits, books about the region and a film highlighting the park. The ¼-mile Fossil Exhibit Trail is one of the park's most popular attractions and is wheelchair accessible. Actual excavation within the park takes place early each summer near the **Conata Basin Picnic Area**; visitors are allowed to watch as workers explore and discover more fossils from prehistoric times.

While visiting the Badlands, be sure to drive South Dakota Hwy. 240, also known as the **Badlands Loop Road**. The 38-mile scenic drive showcases the park's tinted spires and multicolored rock formations, mostly created by wind and water erosion. The road has many pullouts for scenic vistas and offers marked hiking trails. Buffalo, pronghorn antelope, bighorn sheep, mule deer and prairie dogs may be seen throughout the park.

Cedar Pass Lodge, next door to the Ben Reifel Visitor Center, has a gift shop with pottery, beadwork, jewelry and the traditional souvenirs such as postcards, T-shirts and coffee mugs. During the summer, the Lodge's restaurant serves Indian tacos, trout, steaks and buffalo burgers. For lodging within the park, there's a campground and small cabins for rent near Cedar Pass. Call 605-433-5460 or visit www.cedarpasslodge.com for more information. Nearby, the Badlands Inn (605-433-5401) provides modest hotel accommodations.

Breathtaking views of the multicolored rock formations created by wind and water erosion are plentiful in the Badlands National Park south of Wall, SD.

Open year-round; Admission charged.
25216 Ben Reifel Road, P.O. Box 6, Interior, SD 57750
(8 miles south of Wall, SD); 605-433-5361
www.nps.gov/badl/

Neat to Know

➤ **Prairie Homestead** (605-433-5400; www.prairiehome-stead.com) near the east entrance of the Badlands National Park (I-90 Exit 131) is on the National Register of Historic Places and is the only original sod dwelling displayed in South Dakota. Open May through mid-October; Admission is charged.

➤ World-famous **Wall Drug** also offers dinosaur fun (605-279-2175; www.walldrug.com). A life-size brontosaurus greets visitors as they enter town (near I-90, exit 110) and offers a place to stop and picnic with a scenic view of the Badlands. At Wall Drug's Back Yard Mall you'll find an animated roaring T Rex and a smaller cement dinosaur that kids can climb on amid historical gift shops and other family-friendly displays. (For more information see Chapter 9: Wall Drug, page 110.)

EVERYTHING PREHISTORIC AND BLACK HILLS INSTITUTE OF GEOLOGICAL RESEARCH

Dinosaur devotees will be in awe of the large collection of fossils on display at this museum and equally impressed by the extensive offering of fossil- and geology-themed collectibles in the adjacent Everything Prehistoric gift shop. The authentic fossils of Stan, the largest male *Tyrannosaurus rex* ever found, take center stage in the museum display alongside hundreds of fossils from the Cretaceous period, dinosaur eggs and mineral and meteorite collections.

Open year-round; Free admission.
217 Main St., P.O. Box 643, Hill City, SD 57745; 605-574-3919
www.everythingprehistoric.com

MUSEUM OF GEOLOGY

Located on the campus of the South Dakota School of Mines and Technology, this museum collection includes prehistoric mammals, marine reptiles and dinosaurs from the Black Hills and Badlands region, as well as fossils and mineral collections from around the globe. Interpretive paintings hang above the major fossil displays depicting what the animals looked like in prehistoric times. Kids will also enjoy the colorful rock collection, *especially* the fluorescent room with rocks that glow in the dark.

The mosasaur fossils at the Museum of Geology in Rapid City give an up-close view of prehistoric creatures.

Open year-round; Free admission.
501 E. St. Joseph St., Rapid City, SD 57701; 605-394-2467
http://museum.sdsmt.edu

DINOSAUR PARK

Atop Skyline Drive in the center of Rapid City, this unique park features seven enormous replicas of prehistoric reptiles. The park was built in the 1930s and the super-size dinosaurs can be seen from many points in the city. While little ones clamber around these cement Jurassic creatures, adults can marvel at the breathtaking view of the city and surrounding area. The adjacent gift shop offers a variety of dinosaur items from books and toys to T-shirts. Evening lighting gives the statues an eerie glow on the hilltop until 10 pm.

Marvel at the dinosaurs and the view of Rapid City at Dinosaur Park.

Open May to October; Free admission.
940 Skyline Drive, Rapid City, SD 57702; 605-343-8687

FLINTSTONES BEDROCK CITY

Here, children can meet Fred and Barney and ride the Iron Horse train on a tour of the fictional Bedrock City, which includes over a dozen cement buildings. The stone-age setting from dinosaur days gone by includes fun-filled attractions such as Mt. Rockmore, Flintstone cartoons showing in the Rockmore Theatre and an animated performance by the Flintstone Trio. Visitors can also browse the gift shop, snack on Brontoburgers,

Dino Dogs or Chickasaurus ice cream treats. The family can even spend the night at the full-service campground next door (605-673-4664). A playground, heated pool and primitive cabins are also available.

Fred and Barney are happy to greet visitors at Bedrock City near Custer, SD.

Open May to Labor Day; Admission charged.
Highways U.S. 16 and 385, Box 649, Custer, SD 57730; 605-673-4079
www.flintstonesbedrockcity.com

FOR OTHER FOSSILS ON DISPLAY, SEE ALSO:

Chapter 2: Reptile Gardens, Rapid City, page 26

Chapter 5: Journey Museum, Rapid City, page 56; Adams Museum, Deadwood, page 56

Chapter 9: Petrified Forest of the Black Hills, page 113

CHAPTER FOUR

See It Made—Or Mined

Learning is fun with a behind-the-scenes look at how things are made. Or, in the case of the Black Hills' rich gold mining history, seeing how things are mined. Several Black Hills destinations offer tours that mix recreation with education, allowing you to learn how gold was mined, watch jewelry being made and even create your own piece of pottery.

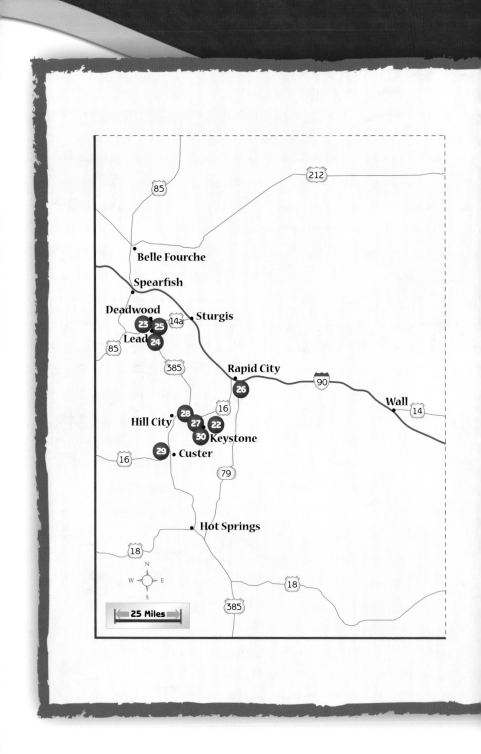

Go For the Gold

More Tours That Teach

BIG THUNDER GOLD MINE

Originally named the Gold Hill Lode, this authentic gold mine was established in 1893. Tours into the mine are handicapped accessible and highlight the history of the mine, Black Hills geology and an extensive display of mining equipment. Gold panning lessons are offered on-site. Amenities include a gift shop and restaurant.

Open May to October; Admission charged.
604 Blair St., P.O. Box 459, Keystone, SD 57751; 605-666-4847 or 800-314-3917

Neat to Know

➤ While in Keystone take a side trip to the **Rushmore Mountain Taffy Shop** (605-666-4430; www.rushmore-mountain-taffy.com) on Main Street where you can watch taffy being made from scratch. Of course, the best part of this "tour" is sampling all the different flavors of taffy.

BROKEN BOOT GOLD MINE

The underground tour of this one-hundred-year-old gold mine showcases the grit and determination of early miners as they burrowed into the earth's rock in search of their fortunes. Narrated tours are given every half hour. Every visitor goes home with a souvenir "share" of stock in the Broken Boot Mine, and you can even pan for gold (outside) with guaranteed results.

Narrated tours at the Broken Boot Gold Mine take visitors into the depths of a real mine at Deadwood.

Open mid-May through mid-September; Admission charged.
Hwy. 14A on upper Main Street, Deadwood, SD 57732; 605-578-1876
www.brokenbootgoldmine.com

HOMESTAKE GOLD MINE VISITOR CENTER

Opened in 1876, the Homestake Mine is the oldest and deepest gold mine in the Western Hemisphere, reaching more than 8,000 feet underground. Although the mine closed in December 2001, surface tours of the Homestake Mining Operation still offer the rare chance to witness the history of American gold mining. The narrated, one-hour bus tour follows the mining process, including hoisting, crushing and milling of the underground ore, viewing Homestake Gold Mine's state-of-the-art waste water treatment plant and seeing the open-cut area that measures 1,250 feet deep and one-half mile across. A gift shop and gold panning are also on-site at the Visitor Center.

Open year-round, tours May through Labor Day only; Admission charged.
160 W. Main Street, P.O. Box 887, Lead, SD 57754; 605-584-3110
www.homestakevisitorcenter.com

BLACK HILLS MINING MUSEUM

Here, a 50-minute *simulated* underground tour provides a comprehensive look at both early and modern underground mining technology used in the Black Hills' Homestake Gold Mine. Also on display in the museum are historical photographs, artifacts and mining equipment. Visitors also have a chance to strike the "mother lode" by panning for their own gold.

Open year-round;
Admission charged.
323 W. Main Street,
P.O. Box 694,
Lead, SD 57754;
605-584-1605
www.mining-
museum.blackhills.com

The Black Hills Mining Museum showcases the region's mining techniques from yesteryear.

Neat to Know: The Story of Black Hills Gold

➤ Legend has it that the inspiration for the Black Hills Gold design dates back to 1876 when a French goldsmith named Henri LeBeau came to the Black Hills to seek his fortune in gold. Unfamiliar with the region, LeBeau became lost, and to avoid starvation found wild grapes to eat. After being rescued, LeBeau realized that this experience was a sign and decided to make his fortune by re-creating grape and leaf clusters in his jewelry designs, which he sold to other miners and prospectors. Today, Black Hills Gold jewelry, with the distinctive tri-color grape cluster and leaf design in pink, green and yellow, can only be manufactured in the Black Hills of South Dakota. It is South Dakota's official state jewelry and is sold throughout the world. Many stores throughout the Hills offer extensive collections of Black Hills gold.

➤ For a special tour showing the region's famous Black Hills gold jewelry being made, visit the following locations. (Note that tours typically last 30 minutes and are only given Monday through Friday.)

Mt. Rushmore Black Hills Gold Factory & Outlet Store
Open year-round; Free admission.
2707 Mt. Rushmore Road (U.S. Hwy. 16),
Rapid City, SD 57709; 605-343-7099 or 800-658-3361
www.mtrushmorejewelry.com

Landstrom's Black Hills Gold Creations
Open year-round; Free admission.
405 Canal Street, Rapid City, SD 57701; 605-343-0157

Stamper Black Hills Gold Jewelry
Tours are not offered, but glass windows in the gift shop allow you to watch artisans create the jewelry.

Open year-round; Free admission.
7201 S. Hwy. 16, Rapid City, SD 57701; 605-342-0751

More Tours That Teach

SIOUX POTTERY

Take a self-guided tour and watch Sioux Indian artisans designing and painting clay pottery, as well as creating dream catchers and other specialty items with bead and quill work. Children receive a free piece of pottery that they can decorate as they sit with a Lakota artist. An adjacent gift shop offers an extensive collection of artists' handcrafted work for sale.

Watch Sioux Indian artisans design and paint clay pottery along with other handcrafts in Rapid City.

Open year-round, tours offered in summer; Free admission.
1441 East St. Joseph, Rapid City, SD 57709; 605-341-3657
www.siouxpottery.com

BLACK HILLS GLASS BLOWERS

Using heat and glass, these artisans create colorful hand-blown works of art, including vases, bowls, animals, ornaments and goblets. The showroom, located one mile west of the only traffic light in Keystone, is open daily during the summer, but glass blowing times are variable. Call ahead to confirm dates of blowing demonstrations.

Open May through September; Free admission.
Old Hill City Road, P.O. Box 703 (1 mile west of Keystone),
Keystone, SD 57751; 605-666-4542

PRAIRIE BERRY WINERY

Opened in May 2004, this facility includes a tasting room and gift shop and offers information about the winemaking process. The family-run winery specializes in using local fruits such as buffaloberry, chokecherry and rhubarb for their award-winning wines under the Prairie Berry label. The winery eventually plans to offer public tours.

Open year-round; Admission charged for tours.
23837 Hwy. 385, P.O. Box 8, Hill City, SD 57745;
605-574-3898 or 877-226-9453
www.prairieberry.com

NATIONAL MUSEUM OF WOODCARVING

This museum includes a carving studio on-site where woodcarvers demonstrate their skill and will transform a block of wood into a piece of art right before your eyes. Other features include a wooden nickel theater and a gallery of work by more than 70 woodcarvers, including one of Disneyland's original animators. Carving times at the museum vary. Call ahead to confirm demonstrations.

Open May to late October; Admission charged.
Hwy. 16 W., P.O. Box 747, Custer, SD 57730; 605-673-4404
www.blackhills.com/woodcarving

THE FRIENDSHIP FACTORY

Here, visitors young and old can make their very own stuffed bear, bunny or other fuzzy animal. The process includes picking out your friend's unstuffed skin, giving it a happy tune or musical sound, stuffing, stitching, fluffing and then dressing and naming it.

Open Memorial Day to Labor Day; Fee charged.
Keystone Mall, Keystone, SD; 605-666-4610

The Badlands near Wall, SD, offer a lesson in wind and water erosion which are said to have created these unique formations. For more about Badlands National Park see page 37.

CHAPTER FIVE

Meaningful Museums

Want to know about the Gold Rush Days in the Black Hills?
Or learn more about the man who carved Mount Rushmore?
Museums throughout the Black Hills tell these and other stories
through an array of exhibits and collections. There's something
to interest everyone, including geology, Native American culture,
the Wild West, gold rush history, homesteading, dolls, motorcycles
and military airplanes to name a few. These tributes to history
give meaning to the region's past and present.

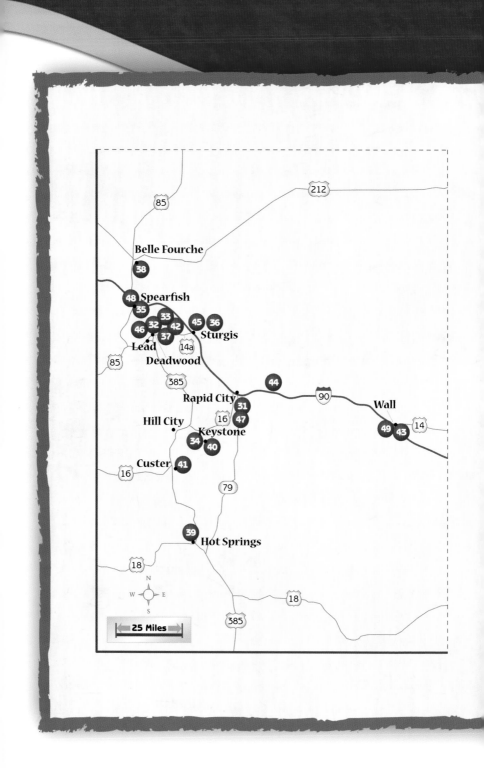

Old West Heritage

Native American Culture

Modern Day Memorabilia

The history of mining, logging, ranching, education and pioneer life have been preserved in the turn of the century artifacts on display at these museums:

THE JOURNEY MUSEUM

This comprehensive museum makes a great starting point for a trek back in time to learn about the earth's geology in the Black Hills region. Chronicling the era of the dinosaur up to the culture of pioneer settlers and Native Americans on the Western Great Plains, exhibits include interactive rock and fossil displays, an archaeology time line and a special fossil dig box for kids. The gift shop features an extensive collection of regional books and Native American art.

Open year-round; Admission charged.
222 New York Street, Rapid City, SD 57709; 605-394-6923
www.journeymuseum.org

ADAMS MUSEUM

Artifacts tied to Deadwood and the Black Hills' pioneer past are on display in the three floors of this historical museum. You'll see a one-of-a-kind plesiosaur fossil, the original Thoen Stone (see Chapter 8, page 114), a replica of one of the largest gold nuggets found in the area and learn about the colorful characters who called Deadwood home. Writers for the HBO series *Deadwood* used the museum's extensive collection of photographs and archival records to lend authenticity to the award-winning drama.

Throughout Deadwood, Wlld Bill Hickock is immortalized in bronze.

Open year-round; Free admission.
54 Sherman Street, Deadwood, SD 57732;
605-578-1714
www.adamsmuseumandhouse.org

THE ADAMS HOUSE

Also in Deadwood, the Adams House is a stately, 1892 Queen Anne-style home with its original furnishings intact. Guided tours detail the history of two of Deadwood's founding families who lived here, including W.E Adams who established the Adams Museum in 1930.

Open year-round; Admission charged.
22 Van Buren Street, Deadwood, SD 57732; 605-578-3724
www.adamsmuseumandhouse.org

BORGLUM HISTORICAL CENTER

This museum collection is dedicated to Gutzon Borglum, the artist who sculpted Mount Rushmore. Carvings and paintings he created during his lifetime are on display, including a replica of Lincoln's titanic eye from the monument. Outside the museum is a duplicate of Borglum's "Seated Lincoln" bronze statue. The original was commissioned in 1910 and sits in front of the Essex County Courthouse in Newark, New Jersey. Children are sure to enjoy climbing on Lincoln's lap for a photo.

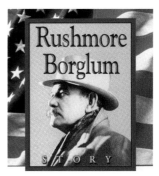

Accomplished artist Gutzon Borglum was a sculptor, painter and American patriot.

Open May through October;
Admission charged.
324 Winter Street, Keystone, SD 57751; 605-666-4448
www.rushmoreborglum.com

Neat to Know

➤ Gutzon Borglum also designed the torch on the Statue of Liberty in New York City.

HIGH PLAINS WESTERN HERITAGE CENTER

Ranch and rodeo memorabilia honor cowboys, pioneers and Native Americans from the region. Also on display are authentic mining and blacksmith artifacts, as well as a Deadwood-Spearfish stagecoach. A Pioneer Room depicts scenes from a completely furnished log cabin and school house as they would have looked a century ago. From its balcony, the museum offers panoramic views of three states—South Dakota, Wyoming and Montana.

Open year-round; Admission charged.
825 Heritage Drive, P.O. Box 524 (I-90, Exit 14), Spearfish, SD 57783;
605-642-9378
www.westernheritagecenter.com

Neat to Know

➤ The High Plains Heritage Center building design is similar to that of the National Cowboy and Western Heritage Museum in Oklahoma City.

FORT MEADE MUSEUM

Established in 1878, this Frontier Post in the Black Hills was home to General George Armstrong Custer's famous Seventh Cavalry. The museum shows a brief film, providing an overview of fort life and the history of Custer's 1874 Black Hills Expedition. It was here that the "Star-Spangled Banner" became the official music for military retreat, long before it became our national anthem. The only survivor of the Little Big Horn, the horse Comanche, was retired with military honors at Fort Meade and lived there for ten years. Be sure to stroll the well-kept military grounds (now home to a veteran's hospital) where some of the Fort's original buildings remain intact. Old Post Cemetery is the only original Cavalry Post Cemetery in the country that has not been moved to a new location. Adjacent to Fort Meade is a Bureau of Land Management recreational area, great for hiking or horseback riding.

To see the fort as it once was, attend the Cavalry Days re-enactment that takes place annually the second weekend in June and includes re-enactments of Civil War history.

Open May 15 to September 15; Admission charged.
Box 164 (one mile east of Sturgis, Hwy. 34), Fort Meade, SD 57741;
605-347-9822
www.fortmeademuseum.org

Neat to Know

➤ **Black Hills National Cemetery** (605-347-3830, www.cem.va.gov/nchp/blackhills.htm) three miles east of Sturgis (I-90 Exit 34) is often called "The Arlington of the West." Dedicated in 1948, simple white headstones mark the final resting places of more than 14,000 veterans and their descendants. The grounds are open daily from sunrise to sunset.

DAYS OF '76 MUSEUM

More than sixty authentic horse-drawn carriages, covered wagons and stagecoaches, including the original Deadwood Stagecoach, are on display here. Located adjacent to the Days of '76 Rodeo grounds, where the annual rodeo is held the third weekend in July.

Open Memorial Day through Labor Day; Free admission.
17 Crescent Street, Deadwood, SD 57732; 605-578-2872

TRI-STATE MEMORIAL MUSEUM

Exhibits include artifacts from early pioneer settlers of the tri-state area of South Dakota, Montana and Wyoming, as well as rodeo history from the region's well-known cowboys. Belle Fourche annually hosts the Black Hills Roundup Rodeo over the Fourth of July.

Open year-round; Free admission.
415 5th Ave., Belle Fourche, SD 57717; 605-723-1200
www.tristatemuseum.com

PIONEER HISTORICAL MUSEUM

Displays showcase the heritage of pioneer living from an early post office and country store to a schoolhouse and dentist office.

Open June through September; Admission charged.
300 North Chicago Street, Hot Springs, SD 57747; 605-745-5147
www.pioneer-museum.com

KEYSTONE HISTORICAL MUSEUM

Housed in the old Keystone school, this museum collection includes a variety of antique furniture and details the gold mining and Mount Rushmore carving history of the area. Memorabilia from Carrie Ingalls (sister of author Laura Ingalls Wilder) is also displayed. Carrie lived in Keystone and operated a newspaper in the early 1900s. The museum even touts a bathtub used by President William Howard Taft.

Open June through August; Free admission.
410 3rd Street, P.O. Box 177,
Keystone, SD 57751; 605-255-5280
www.keystonehistory.com

Neat to Know

> ➤ The **"Old Town" Keystone Walking Tour** features 19 historical points from Keystone's early years. Sights include a log school house, an ice house and the mercantile store. Brochures with information about each point are available at the **Keystone Museum**; each site has information panels.

CUSTER COUNTY 1881 COURTHOUSE MUSEUM

This original courthouse and jail features photos from General Custer's 1874 Expedition along with historical mining, Native American and schoolhouse artifacts.

The stately 1881 Courthouse Museum overlooks Custer's Main Street.

Open May through September; Admission charged.
411 Mt. Rushmore Road, Box 826, Custer, SD 57730; 605-673-2443
www.1881courthousemuseum.com

Neat to Know: How about an "Old Time" Photo?

➤ If your museum trek has made you wild about life in the west a hundred years ago, try capturing the moment by posing for an old time photo. Several small studios throughout the Black Hills specialize in recreating the Wild West in vintage portraits with you as the star. Costumes range from hardy pioneers, dance hall girls, to a law-abiding sheriff or blushing bride. Youngsters look quite cute sitting in a washtub. Some studios will even take portraits with you and your motorcycle or a special automobile.

Studios include:

Woody's Wild West Old Time Photo
Open year-round.
641 Main Street, Deadwood, 57732; 605-578-3807
www.woodyswildwest.com

"Old Time" Photo, continued

Boondocks

Step back into the 1950s at Boondocks with its Rock-n-Roll theme, old-fashioned diner serving authentic burgers and malts, a collection of classic cars and studebakers, and a drive-in studio for vintage portraits of people, motorcycles and cars.

Open May to early-October.
Highway 385 (9 miles south of Deadwood), Deadwood, SD 57732;
605-578-1186
www.fiftiesfun.com

Buffalo Old Time Photo Co.

Open May through September.
220 Winter Street (on Main Street), Keystone, SD 57751; 605-666-4473
www.buffalophoto.net

Professor Samuel's

Open April to mid-October.
118 Winter Street (on Main Street), Keystone, SD 57751;
605-666-4761 or 605-343-4267
www.professorsamuels.com

GoodTyme Photo

Open May to Labor Day.
804 Hwy. 16A, Keystone, SD 57751; 605-666-4619

Key Photo

Open year-round.
241 Winter Street (next to Borglum Historical Center),
Keystone, SD 57751; 605-666-4311

Looking Back Photo Co.

Open Memorial Day to Labor Day.
409 Main Street, Hill City, SD 57745; 605-574-3314

Frontier Photo

Open year-round.
512 Mt. Rushmore Road, Custer, SD 57730; 605-673-2269
www.frontierphotos.com

Legacy Old Time Photo

Open May through September, appointment recommended.
525 Main Street, Wall, SD 57790; 605-279-2882
www.blackhillsbadlands.com/legacy/

TATANKA: STORY OF THE BISON

The centerpiece of this scenic mountaintop is a larger-than-life bronze statue of 14 bison being pursued over a cliff by three Native American horseback riders. Sculpted by South Dakota artist Peggy Detmers, Tatanka is the third-largest bronze sculpture in the world and was commissioned by actor Kevin Costner who filmed his award-winning *Dances With Wolves* in South Dakota.

Bronze buffalo amidst Native American horseback riders are breathtaking atop this Black Hills mountain near Deadwood.

Displays in the visitor center tell the story of the bison on the Northern Plains through photographs and artifacts. Lakota Indian presenters teach visitors about the importance of the bison to their way of life over 150 years ago. A snack bar and Native American gift shop are also on site.

Open April to October; Admission charged.
100 Tatanka Drive, P.O. Box 503, U.S. Highway 85 (one mile north
of Deadwood), Deadwood, SD 57732; 605-584-5678
www.storyofthebison.com

Neat to Know

➤ The **Vore Buffalo Jump** (3½ miles west of Beulah, WY) is a natural sinkhole used by Plains Indians between 1500 and 1800 AD as a big game kill site—stampeding herds of buffalo over the cliff to their death.

Archaeologists say the remains of 20,000 bison are likely to be excavated at the Vore Jump. Presently, the site is open to the public during summer months and donations are encouraged. A research, education and cultural center is eventually planned at the location. From I-90 take Exit 205 or Exit 199.

WOUNDED KNEE: THE MUSEUM

This museum is dedicated to telling the story of the Wounded Knee Massacre, which occurred in 1890 as a small band of Lakota families fled through the landscape trying to reach the protection of the Pine Ridge Agency in southwestern South Dakota. Exhibits detail the life of the Lakota as it was impacted by U.S. military operations. A Children's Corner includes displays about Lakota children, Lakota culture and how the Lakota people chose their names.

A marker at the Wounded Knee gravesite pays tribute to the Lakota who lost their lives.

Open Memorial Day through Labor Day; Admission charged.
207 10th Ave., P.O. Box 348, I-90 Exit 110, Wall, SD 57790; 605-279-2573
www.woundedkneemuseum.org

Modern Day Memorabilia

SOUTH DAKOTA AIR AND SPACE MUSEUM

With 28 aircraft, historical bombers and missiles on display, you'll get a real-life feel for air and space history. Highlights include a modern day B-1 bomber, General Eisenhower's personal B-25 transport from World War II and a Minuteman II Missile Launch Control Center. Bus tours of Ellsworth Air Force Base and a minuteman missile silo are also offered for a nominal fee and depart from the museum daily from mid-May to mid-September. Aviation items are available for sale in the gift shop.

Just one of the 28 aircraft, bombers and missiles on display at the Air and Space Museum adjacent to Ellsworth Air Force Base.

Open year-round; Free admission.
P.O. Box 871, I-90 Exit 67B, (7 miles east of Rapid City next to Ellsworth Air Force Base), Box Elder, SD 57719; 605-385-5188

Neat to Know

➤ For a glimpse of Cold War history, tours are offered of the **Minuteman Missile National Historic Site** (605-433-5552, www.nps.gov/mimi) located 20 miles east of Wall (I-90 Exit 131). The two-hour tours are given twice daily from Memorial Day through Labor Day and can also be arranged in the off-season. Tours are complimentary, but reservations are necessary.

STURGIS MOTORCYCLE MUSEUM AND HALL OF FAME

As host to the Sturgis Motorcycle Rally and Races held early each August, it is fitting that Sturgis is also home to a museum dedicated to motorcycles. On display you'll see rare and extraordinary motorcycles and scooters from the early 1900s through the present. With over 100 motorcycles in its collection, displays are rotated regularly, offering repeat visitors something new every time they stop in.

During August, Sturgis is a mecca for motorcyclists from around the world.

Open year-round; Admission charged.
999 Main Street, P.O. Box 605, Sturgis, SD 57785; 605-347-2001
www.sturgismuseum.com

Neat to Know

➤ In 1938, Sturgis hosted its first dirt-track motorcycle race, which evolved into one of the world's largest annual motorcycle rallies.

➤ On your way to or from the Black Hills from the east, consider a stop at the **Pioneer Auto Show** along I-90 at Murdo, South Dakota. Over 250 collectible cars, motorcycles and antique tractors are on display—including the General Lee from the *Dukes of Hazzard*. For more information visit www.pioneerautoshow.com or call 605-669-2691. Open year-round; Admission charged.

CELEBRITY HOTEL, NELSON'S GARAGE CAR AND MOTORCYCLE MUSEUM, AND THE MINT

Throughout the main floor of this hotel and casino are authentic movie props, costumes and vehicles, including James Bond's Aston Martin, Herbie the Love Bug, Evel Knievel's motorcycle and more.

Additional movie memorabilia can be found across the street from the Celebrity Hotel at **The Mint**, where John Wayne's pickup and prop guns used in classic Western movies are displayed.

Open year-round; Free admission.
629 Main Street, Deadwood, SD 57732; 605-578-1909 or 888-399-1886
www.celebritycasinos.com

Neat to Know: Movie Mementos

➤ Also on Main Street in Deadwood, the **Midnight Star** (605-578-1555 or 800-999-6482), owned by actor Kevin Costner, showcases collectibles from his career. The second level of the building operates as Diamond Lil's Sports Bar and Grill, its walls filled with displays of photos, costumes, props and movie posters.

THE DAHL ARTS CENTER

History surrounds visitors as they view the Dahl's unique 180-foot oil-on-canvas panorama that spans 200 years of the United States' past. Painted by muralist Bernard Thomas, special lighting and narration tell of America's birth on the East Coast to its westward expansion and development as a country. Additional exhibits and galleries focus on contemporary art. **The Black Hills Community Theatre** performances are hosted from September through May in the 170-seat theater (for more information, see Chapter 9, page 123.) Special children's shows, educational classes and camps are offered in the summer.

Open year-round, closed Mondays; Free admission.
713 7th St., Rapid City, SD 57701; 605-394-4101
www.thedahl.org

Cyclorama is a 180-foot panorama depicting 200 years of U.S. economic history.

DOLLS AT HOME MUSEUM

A dollhouse village, miniature furniture and dolls of all sizes adorn this unique collection. Most of the items belong to Johanna Meier, whose family founded Spearfish's well-known **Black Hills Passion Play** (see Chapter 9, page 122). Meier has added to her collection during her travels around the world as an international opera singer. Also on display is a First Lady Doll Collection, which includes doll-size replicas of nearly all of the First Ladies in their inaugural gowns.

Open daily, Memorial Day through Labor Day and by appointment;
Admission charged.
435 Meyer Ave., Spearfish, SD 57783; 605-645-2192
www.blackhills.com/bhpp/pp_index.htm

NATIONAL GRASSLANDS VISITOR CENTER

Here you'll learn about the prairie plants, animals and natural resources that surround the Badlands area and make up the Buffalo Gap National Grasslands. Great Plains history, grasslands management and recreational activities on the National Grasslands are also detailed through interpretive displays and videos about the region.

Open year-round; Free admission.
708 Main Street, P.O. Box 425, Wall, SD 57790; 605-279-2125

Neat to Know

> ➤ **The Wildlife Museum** (605-279-2418) located on Wall's Main Street showcases a diverse collection of animals from the region and around the world. Open mid-May through October; Admission charged.

FOR MORE MUSEUM COLLECTIONS, SEE ALSO

Chapter 1: Lincoln Borglum Museum, Keystone, page 13; National Presidential Wax Museum, Keystone, page 14; Indian Museum of North America at Crazy Horse, Custer, page 17; Saloon No. 10, Deadwood, page 21; Wild West Wax Museum, Wall, page 21

Chapter 3: Everything Prehistoric and Black Hills Institute of Geological Research, Hill City, page 39; Museum of Geology, Rapid City, page 39

Chapter 4: Black Hills Mining Museum, Lead, page 47; National Museum of Woodcarving, Custer, page 50

CHAPTER SIX

Outdoors to Explore

If you like to hike, bike, horseback ride, fish, camp—or simply relax—the Black Hills is the perfect place to enjoy the great outdoors. The beauty of the Black Hills National Forest is the backdrop for peaceful settings like the Mickelson Trail, Custer State Park, Spearfish Canyon and the nearby natural wonders of Bear Butte and Devils Tower. No matter the season, they afford an endless variety of scenery and activities.

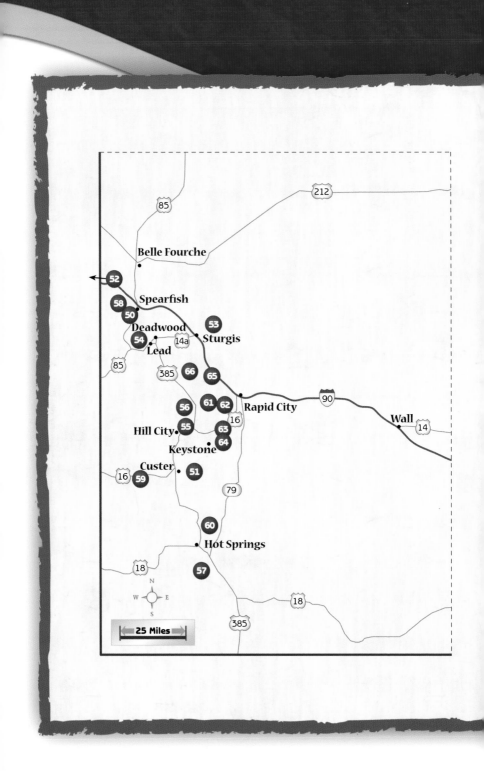

Scenic Settings

Lakes You'll Love

Cavernous Curiosities

Biking, Skiing and More

SPEARFISH CANYON

This picturesque canyon stretches for twenty miles along Spearfish Creek and is framed by towering canyon walls of rich, red sandstone. With each changing season, the canyon presents a new perspective: rejuvenation in spring, tranquility in summer, color in fall and serenity in winter. Frank Lloyd Wright visited the sight in 1933 and said, "had Spearfish Canyon been on the 'throughway' to westward migration, the canyon would be as significant in public appreciation as the Grand Canyon is today."

The Canyon's Highway 14A is a National Scenic Byway that winds between Spearfish Canyon Golf Course and historic Deadwood. There are many turnouts for taking photos along the way, and sightseers are joined by fishermen, picnickers, bicyclers, joggers and hikers throughout the canyon.

Several waterfalls throughout Spearfish Canyon make it a picture perfect setting.

Making your way along the highway, **Bridal Veil Falls** will catch your eye with its cascading water over the face of a 40-foot-high cliff. At **Savoy**, Latchstring Village includes a restaurant and the stately **Spearfish Canyon Lodge** (605-584-3435, 877-YR-LODGE; www.spfcanyon.com) Depending on the season, bicycles or snowmobiles can be rented at the resort. Creeks within the canyon offer year-round fishing; fly fishing guides can also be arranged through the Lodge.

A marked hiking trail that begins behind Latchstring Inn descends toward the creek and reveals breathtaking views of **Spearfish Falls**. West of Savoy and up Little Spearfish Canyon, **Roughlock Falls** is a popular picnic and hiking spot. About a mile beyond Roughlock Falls is the site where several scenes for the movie *Dances With Wolves* were filmed.

Accessible year-round.
Hwy. 14A, Spearfish, SD 57783

Neat to Know

➤ Along Spearfish Canyon at the intersection of Hwy. 85 and Hwy. 14A is **Cheyenne Crossing** (605-584-3510), so named because it is the point where the old Cheyenne Trail crossed Spearfish Creek. This is a popular stop for its gift shop and restaurant that serves up homemade pancakes, Indian tacos and burgers for big appetites. Open daily, May to October. Next door, **Wickiup Village** (605-584-3382, 800-505-8268; www.spearfishcreekcabins.com) offers log cabins for rent year-round.

CUSTER STATE PARK

Hiking, mountain biking, rock climbing, swimming, canoeing, paddle boating, trail rides and miles of scenic vistas are just a few of the many reasons visitors call Custer State Park a favorite.

Initially established as a game reserve in 1913, the area was deemed Custer State Park in 1919 by former South Dakota Governor Peter Norbeck. Today the visitor center and the 70-mile **Peter Norbeck Scenic Byway,** which encircles the park and showcases much of its natural beauty, bear his name.

To get to know this vast park, start with a stop at the **Peter Norbeck Visitor Center** where you can pick up maps and learn about the many trails, nature areas and lakes. For overnight stays, there are seven campsites and four resorts within Custer State Park—some even offer cabins year-round. Reservations are necessary. Call 800-710-2267 for camping and 800-658-3530 for the resorts.

Open year-round, Admission charged.
HC 83, Box 70, Custer, SD 57730; 605-255-4515
www.custerstatepark.info

FAVORITE HIKING TRAILS WITHIN CUSTER STATE PARK

If hiking is your fancy, panoramic views are offered atop many hiking trails within Custer State Park.

Most popular is the trek to the top of **Harney Peak**, the state's highest elevation at 7,242 feet. The tallest mountain between the Rockies and the Swiss Alps, Harney's summit affords a panoramic view of four states. Trail 9 and Trail 4 at **Sylvan Lake** both lead to Harney Peak. Trail 9, which is 3 miles one-way, is the most traveled and considered the easiest route. Trail 4, which is 3¼ miles one-way, goes from Sylvan Lake to the **Little Devils Tower** trailhead and then on toward Harney Peak. Round trip on either of these trails, the hike takes about 4 hours and is moderately strenuous.

Harney Peak is South Dakota's tallest mountain at 7,242 feet.

Other favorite trails (listed by level of difficulty) include:

- **EASY: These trails mainly follow level ground.**

Sylvan Lake Shore Trail: This 1-mile loop encircles Sylvan Lake. Most of the trail is flat, but a portion crosses rocky areas.

Creekside Trail is a 2-mile, paved, handicapped accessible trail that follows Grace Coolidge Creek between the State Game Lodge and Coolidge General Store.

- **MODERATE: Parts of these trails follow steep slopes and rocky areas.**

Badger Clark Historic Trail: Located behind the historic Badger Hole, this trail makes a 1-mile loop through the forest and rocky hillside.

Prairie Trail: Making a 3-mile loop off the Wildlife Loop Road, this trail features the prairie grasslands and wildflowers.

Stockade Lake Trail begins on the southeast side of Stockade Lake and ascends to a ridgeline where excellent views of the area can be seen. This trail makes a 1½-mile loop.

Little Devils Tower Trailhead begins 1 mile east of Sylvan Lake on Needles Hwy. The 3-mile one-way trail leads to the unique rock formation known as Little Devils Tower. The summit also provides beautiful views of the Cathedral Spires and Harney Peak.

- **STRENUOUS: Much of these trails follow steep slopes and rocky areas.**

Sunday Gulch Trail begins behind the dam at Sylvan Lake and follows a 2⅘-mile loop into the forest. This challenging trail offers spectacular scenery of granite walls and streams.

Lovers Leap Trail is a popular trail that begins behind the schoolhouse across from the Peter Norbeck Visitor Center. This trail makes a 3-mile loop and follows the top of a ridgeline, with a rocky outcrop at the highest point called Lovers Leap. Mount Coolidge, Harney Peak and the Cathedral Spires can be viewed from this high point. The trail does include some creek crossings which can be challenging.

Cathedral Spires Trail is a one-way, 1½-mile trail to the rugged granite spires. The trailhead begins 2½ miles east of Sylvan Lake on Needles Hwy.

The Black Hills' Cathedral Spires earned their name because the granite outcroppings look like the pipes of a church organ.

CULTURE IN CUSTER

Cultural activities within Custer State Park include **The Badger Hole**, the historic log cabin home of Charles Badger Clark (1883-1957), South Dakota's first poet laureate. After a cabin tour, hike the Badger Clark Historic Trail and reflect at quiet stops among the pines.

At the **Gordon Stockade** near Stockade Lake, a replica of the log fort built by the Gordon party, who came to this area in search of gold in 1874, is a reminder of the early Gold Rush days.

Also during the summer, the **Black Hills Playhouse** offers live theater productions nightly in the park. Performances begin at 8 pm. Call 605-255-4141 for tickets.

RESORTS AND RECREATION

The park's four resorts are hubs of activity with everything from boating and swimming to the Buffalo Safari Jeep Rides and chuckwagon cookouts. Each of the four resorts in Custer State Park also offer their own unique restaurants with food from casual burgers to upscale trout, pheasant and buffalo.

Sylvan Lake Resort (605-574-2561) is a popular attraction because of the soothing lake of the same name nearby. Here, visitors can picnic, swim, fish, climb among the granite rocks, meander along the trail that encircles Sylvan Lake or hike one of the many trailheads that begin here. This stately lodge was influenced by Frank Lloyd Wright. In addition to the restaurant and lodge rooms, amenities include cabins for rent, a campground, a convenience store and row boat and paddle boat rentals.

Scenic Sylvan Lake is a favorite Black Hills destination.

Legion Lake Resort (605-255-4521) is located on the water's edge and offers fishing, boat rentals and a sandy beach for lounging. You can rent cabins here, as well as paddle boats, hydrobikes and mountain bikes for use on the nearby Centennial Trail. You can even pick up a fishing license and supplies.

Blue Bell Lodge and Resort (605-255-4531) is known for its western flair—including guided trail rides, hayrides and chuckwagon cookouts where guests get a cowboy hat and bandana as a souvenir. Some cabins are available year-round.

The historic **State Game Lodge and Resort** (605-255-4541) was nicknamed the "Summer White House" after hosting Presidents Coolidge and Eisenhower. Buffalo Safari Jeep Rides leave from the Lodge allowing visitors to get into the park backcountry. Fly-fishing trips and mountain bike rentals are available, and some cabins are available year-round.

For more about the wildlife within Custer State Park, see Chapter 2, page 28.

Neat to Know: More About Custer State Park

➤ U.S. Highway 16A, also known as the **Iron Mountain Road**, provides spectacular views of Mount Rushmore and the Black Hills. The winding mountain road features three tunnels that were constructed specifically to frame views of Mount Rushmore, as well as the famous corkscrew bridges called the "pigtails."

➤ Two geological features in Custer State Park include the famous **Needles Eye** and the **Cathedral Spires**, which can be viewed along Needles Highway. These outcrops are made of granite. Viewed at the right angle, Needles Eye appears to be a gigantic sewing needle. Cathedral Spires give the impression of gigantic organ pipes set into the mountain scenery.

➤ The **Mount Coolidge Lookout and Fire Tower** was built in 1940 by the Civilian Conservation Corps atop a 6,023-foot peak. It is used for communications and for spotting fires. Visitors can hike or drive to the top of Mount Coolidge and then climb the lookout tower that provides views of Mount Rushmore, Crazy Horse Memorial, Harney Peak, the Needles formations and—on a clear day—the Badlands over 60 miles away. The turnoff to the tower is on SD Hwy. 87 where a 1$\frac{7}{10}$ mile gravel road winds up the mountain. This road is not suited to large vehicles or motor homes.

➤ The **French Creek Natural Area** and **Grace Coolidge Walk-In Fishing Area** have been designated as natural areas and will be left untouched by human development. They offer great fishing and wildlife viewing.

➤ Custer State Park's **Coolidge General Store** was built in 1927 by shipbuilders from Minnesota to accommodate the entourage of staff, reporters and curious tourists that followed President Coolidge when he stayed at the park's State Game Lodge that summer. Inside the store, be sure to look up—the builders used their ingenuity to craft a ceiling that resembles the hull of a ship turned upside down.

DEVILS TOWER NATIONAL MONUMENT

In 1906, President Teddy Roosevelt designated the 1,267-foot-tall Devils Tower as the nation's first national monument. This unique structure is actually the core of a volcano exposed after millions of years of erosion. A 1½-mile, paved walking path encircles the base of the tower. The area also offers marked hiking trails, rock climbing (by permit), summer cultural programs and camping.

Monument open year-round; Visitor Center open April through November; Admission charged.
P.O. Box 10 (9 miles west of Hulett, WY),
Devils Tower, WY 82714;
307-467-5283
www.nps.gov/deto

Just across the border in Wyoming, Devils Tower was the nation's first national monument.

Neat to Know: The Legend of Devils Tower

➤ Native American lore says the mountain was created when seven small girls, chased by a bear, jumped on a rock and prayed to the rock to save them. The rock heard their pleas and began to rise upward, pushing them higher, out of reach of the bear. The bear clawed and jumped at the sides of the mountain, but broke its claws and fell to the ground. The little girls were pushed up into the sky where they remain to this day in a group of seven little stars—the Pleiades. The marks of the bear claws are seen as the vertical ridges on Devils Tower.

➤ The Black Hills is quickly becoming recognized for the **outstanding rock climbing** its granite spires offer. Favorite formations for climbers to conquer include Devils Tower National Monument near Hulett, WY, The Needles in Custer State Park, granite peaks near Mount Rushmore and limestone cliffs in Spearfish Canyon. A longtime guide service in the region is **Sylvan Rocks**, 208 Main, Hill City, SD 57745; 605-574-2425, www.sylvanrocks.com

BEAR BUTTE STATE PARK

Considered sacred ground by Native Americans, Bear Butte stands alone on the plains east of Sturgis. Mato Paha, or bear mountain, is the Lakota name given to this unique formation, which is not a flat-topped butte as its name implies, but rather a single mountain rising from the surrounding prairie.

Native Americans revere Bear Butte near Sturgis as sacred ground.

Bear Butte's history includes serving as a landmark that helped guide settlers and gold prospectors into the region after General George Custer camped near the mountain and verified rumors of gold in the Black Hills. Today, Bear Butte State Park has been designated as a National Natural Landmark and a National Recreation Trail. The popular hiking trail winds nearly two miles up to the summit of Bear Butte, where you'll discover a breathtaking view of four states. During your hike, you may also get glimpses of native wildlife and the small herd of buffalo that roams at the base of the mountain.

Near the entrance to the park, the Bear Butte Education Center offers interpretive displays about the geological story of this almost-volcano, its cultural significance as a pioneer landmark and its continuing role as a holy mountain for several Indian tribes. A small lake across the highway from Bear Butte offers a pretty setting for a picnic. Campsites, a boat ramp and a handicapped accessible fishing dock are also available.

Open year-round; Admission charged.
Box 688, Sturgis, SD 57785; 605-347-5240
www.sdgfp.info/Parks/Regions/NorthernHills/BearButte.htm

Neat to Know: Sacred Ground

> ➤ The Black Hills were named Paha Sapa, meaning "hills black" by the Lakota Indians because the pine covered slopes look black from a distance. Indians revere the Hills as a sacred, holy place where the great spirits live. Notable leaders including **Red Cloud**, **Crazy Horse** and **Sitting Bull** have all visited Bear Butte, and many Native Americans still hold religious ceremonies on the mountain. During your visit, you may see colorful prayer cloths and tobacco ties hanging from the trees that represent the prayers offered by individuals during their worship.

> ➤ Bear Butte State Park is linked to Custer State Park and Wind Cave National Park by the 111-mile **Centennial Trail** that winds through the Black Hills. It is open to hiking, mountain biking, horseback riding and cross-country skiing.

GEORGE S. MICKELSON TRAIL

Named for the late South Dakota Governor who supported it, the 109-mile Mickelson Trail winds through the heart of the Black Hills following the historic Burlington Northern Rail Line from Deadwood to Edgemont. Passing pine trees, granite outcrops, stands of aspen and spruce, quiet meadows and gurgling streams, the trail is popular with hikers, cyclists and horseback riders. It is also a favorite for cross-country skiing or snowshoeing in winter.

The Mickelson Trail stretches over 100 miles from Deadwood to Edgemont.

The trail includes 14 trailheads and a mix of gentle to extreme slopes, tunnels and bridges amid the beautiful back-country. The trail winds through several towns (and ghost towns) with 30 interpretive signs along the way to explain special features. For bicycle rentals, see page 87.

Accessible year-round, A user fee is charged.
11361 Nevada Gulch Road, Lead, SD 57754; 605-584-3896
www.MickelsonTrail.com

Neat to Know: Find Nemo

➤ The scenery is breathtaking in the peaceful valley that surrounds the tiny town of Nemo, in the heart of the Black Hills National Forest. Nemo was the site of William Randolf Hearst's first logging operation in 1876, which supplied lumber to the Homestake Mine in Lead. **Nemo Guest Ranch** (605-578-2708; www.nemoguestranch.com) offers cabins, RV hookups and campsites. Located on Nemo Road, off Hwy. 385, south of Deadwood.

Nemo Guest Ranch is a quaint setting for a picnic or camping.

FOR MORE AREAS TO HIKE AND EXPLORE, SEE ALSO

Chapter 3: Badlands National Park, page 37

Lakes You'll Love

Many picturesque lakes are found throughout the Black Hills, offering family fun for fishing, swimming and boating. **Sylvan Lake** and **Legion Lake** within Custer State Park have already been mentioned in this chapter. Other popular spots include:

SHERIDAN LAKE

Located north of Hill City beside Hwy. 385, Sheridan Lake is the second-largest in the Black Hills National Forest. It has a sandy, west-facing beach that many consider the sunniest in the Hills. The area offers two camp-grounds, three picnic areas, hiking trails (including the Flume Trail and Centennial Trail) and ample fishing. Pontoon boats, canoes, paddle boats and kayak rentals are available. Sheridan Lake Marina operates from late April to mid-October. Some ice fishing is done in January and February.

Hill City, SD, Marina; 605-574-2169

PACTOLA RESERVOIR

At 860 acres, Pactola Reservoir is the largest lake in the Black Hills and is up to 158 feet deep. The man-made lake is backed up behind Pactola Dam and used for flood control on Rapid Creek, which flows through Rapid City. The Pactola Visitor Center, just south of the dam on Hwy. 385, provides a scenic overlook of the lake and information about the Black Hills National Forest (open Memorial Day through Labor Day). The lake has two marinas with boat ramps and offers pontoon and fishing boat rentals. Two picnic grounds and two campgrounds are also located on the lake. Pactola Pines Marina is open from April 15 through October 15, with limited hours before Memorial Day and after Labor Day.

Pactola Reservoir is the largest lake in the Black Hills. It is man-made.

Rapid City, SD, Marina; 605-343-4283

ANGOSTURA RESERVOIR RECREATION AREA

This man-made lake is a water-lover's haven with ample room for boating, fishing and swimming, as well as 36 miles of shoreline with some of the finest sandy beaches in South Dakota. The site is a great spot for picnics and includes playgrounds, hiking and biking trails. Cabin rentals and campground are available on-site.

Open year-round; Admission charged.
HC 52, Box 131-A (10 miles southeast of Hot Springs off Hwy. 385),
Hot Springs, SD 57747; 605-745-6996
www.recreation.gov/detail.cfm?ID=1161

IRON CREEK LAKE

This quiet lake in the northern Black Hills offers a sandy beach, swimming, fishing and paddle boat rentals. Hiking, biking and volleyball are popular, as are the rustic cabins and primitive campground.

10438 W. Hwy. 14, Spearfish, SD 57783; 605-642-5851
www.ironcreeklake.com

OTHER LAKES AND STREAMS

Smaller lakes with campgrounds include **Roubaix Lake**, south of Deadwood off Hwy. 385, and **Horsethief Lake** along Hwy. 244, near Mount Rushmore.

Orman Dam, east of Belle Fourche, SD, on Hwy. 212, and **Keyhole State Park**, southwest of Devils Tower in Wyoming, off I-90, offer large reservoirs for fishing, boating and watersports. **Stockade Lake** in Custer State Park also offers a boat ramp.

Rainbow trout are the most abundant in Black Hills lakes, while brown and brook trout are mostly in streams. **Deerfield Lake**, 15 miles northwest of Hill City, boasts some of the best trout fishing in the Black Hills. Among the most popular trout fishing streams are fast-flowing **Rapid Creek**, **French Creek** and spring-fed **Spearfish Creek**. Fishing licenses are required at all public fishing areas.

Neat to Know: Catch of the Day

➤ For guaranteed fishing success, cast your line at **Trout Haven** (605-833-2571 or www.blackhillsattractions.com) located 20 miles south of Deadwood and 19 miles west of Rapid City on Hwy. 385. No license is needed; they even furnish the fishing rod and bait. The experience is fun for all ages, and the Pier Café will fry your catch immediately or pack your trout on ice to go. Open Memorial Day to Labor Day; September weekends only.

Want to know what the Black Hills is really made of? Get an in-depth geology lesson with an underground tour of one of the region's eight caves. A ring of limestone encircles the land beneath the Hills to create the second-largest cave system in the world. All of the caves offer guided, public tours showcasing rare underground crystal formations such as stalactites, stalagmites, boxwork and cave popcorn. These caverns make an especially good place to visit on bad-weather days or extremely hot days, because most stay a constant temperature of about 50 degrees.

JEWEL CAVE NATIONAL MONUMENT

With over 133 miles of known passageways, Jewel Cave, so named because of the jewel-like crystals that line its walls, is the third-longest in the world. Operated by the National Park Service, scenic tunnel tours are given several times daily. During the summer months, special lantern and spelunking tours are offered. These are longer tours and reservations are required. Hiking is also offered on two surface trails at the national monument.

Jewel Cave, near Custer, is the third-longest cave in the world.

Open year-round, Admission charged.
RR1 Box 60 AA (12 miles west of Custer on Hwy. 16), Custer, SD 57730;
605-673-2288
www.nps.gov/jeca

WIND CAVE NATIONAL PARK

Named for the strong wind currents that blow alternately in and out of the cave, Wind Cave offers five different tours of its extensive passageways. Less strenuous tours are ½ mile long, while longer tours last from two to four hours and include as many as 450 stairs.

Above ground, Wind Cave is surrounded by 28,000 acres of native grasslands and Ponderosa pine forests, offering 30 miles of hiking trails and camping and picnic areas. The **Rankin Ridge Trail** (1¼ miles long) offers a panoramic view of the Black Hills from the fire lookout tower at its summit. The park can be accessed from Hwy. 385 10 miles north of Hot Springs or on Hwy. 87 from Custer State Park.

Open year-round,
Admission charged.
RR1 Box 190,
Hot Springs, SD 57747;
605-745-4600
www.nps.gov/wica

With five different tours offered, there's something for everyone at Wind Cave.

BLACK HILLS CAVERNS

Over a dozen different crystal formations from nailhead spar crystal to soda straw stalactites are featured on these guided tours.

Open May 1 to September 30; Admission charged.
2600 Cavern Road (4 miles west of Rapid City on Hwy. 44),
Rapid City, SD 57702; 605-343-0542 or 800-837-9358
www.blackhillscaverns.com

CRYSTAL CAVE PARK

Forty-minute tours are offered and are said to be the least strenuous of all of the Black Hills cave tours. Highlights include 16 different types of formations, including the rare "birdbaths."

Open May through September; Admission charged.
7700 Nameless Cave Road (1 mile west of Rapid City on Hwy. 44,
then 2 miles into entrance), Rapid City, SD 57702; 605-342-8008
www.southdakotacaves.com/crystal_cave.htm

Neat to Know

➤ Farther west of Crystal Cave Park and Black Hills Caverns on Hwy. 44 (10 miles west of Rapid City) is another underground marvel—a waterfall. Located 600 feet inside an old Black Hills gold mine, **Thunderhead Underground Falls** is a one-of-a-kind experience. The hike to the waterfall is easily accessible. For information call 605-343-0081 or visit www.blackhillsbadlands.com/thfalls. Open May through October; Admission charged.

SITTING BULL CRYSTAL CAVERNS

Tours last approximately 45 minutes and feature dog-tooth spar crystals. The gift shop includes Native American beadwork and jewelry.

Open May through October; Admission charged.
13745 South Hwy. 16 (9 miles south of Rapid City), Rapid City, SD 57701; 605-342-2777
www.sittingbullcrystalcave.com

BEAUTIFUL RUSHMORE CAVE

This easily accessible cave is the closest to Mount Rushmore and provides child carriers for small children.

Open May 1 to October 31; Admission charged.
13622 Highway 40 (6 miles east of Keystone), Keystone, SD 57751; 605-255-4467 or 605-255-4384
www.beautifulrushmorecave.com

View amazing stalactites at Beautiful Rushmore Cave near Keystone.

STAGEBARN CRYSTAL CAVE

Open Memorial Day through Labor Day, Admission charged.
10829 Stagebarn Road (11 miles north of Rapid City, 2 miles off of I-90; follow signs at Exit 48), Piedmont, SD 57769; 605-787-6606
www.blackhillsattractions.com/pages/attractions/stagebarncrystalcave.html

WONDERLAND CAVE PARK

Located in the heart of the Black Hills National Forest, it's a scenic drive to reach this historic cave, which has been open to the public since 1929.

Open May 1 through September; Admission charged.
Take I-90 Exit 32 at Sturgis and follow signs along Vanocker Canyon Road, Nemo, SD 57759; 605-578-1728
www.southdakotacaves.com/wonderland_cave.htm

Biking, Skiing and More

BICYCLE RENTALS

For a bicycle tour of the Hills, rentals are available at several locations, primarily along the 109-mile Mickelson Trail (see page 80). Many offer tour packages and shuttle services with drop-off and pick-up points.

ROCHFORD RIDERS

Rentals and shuttles, also kids' bikes and trailers for little tykes.
Open May to November 1.
Rochford, SD 57778; 605-584-3868

DEADWOOD BICYCLES

Open May through September.
180 Sherman Street, Deadwood, SD 57732; 605-578-1345
www.deadwoodbicycles.com

PRESIDENTS PARK

Open year-round, Bike rentals and shuttles, May through September.
11249 Presidents Park Loop, Lead, SD 57754; 605-584-9925
www.presidentspark.com

RABBIT BICYCLE

Open April to October; Occasional shuttle service.
(across from the 1880 Train entrance) Hill City, SD 57745; 605-381-1555

FORT WE-LIKE-IT CAMPGROUND

Open May through September; Moped rentals also available.
24992 Sylvan Lake Road, Hwy. 89, Custer, SD 57730;
605-673-3600 or 888-946-2267
www.blackhillsrv.com

CUSTER STATE PARK

Rentals available May through September at:
Legion Lake Resort *605-255-4521*
State Game Lodge and Resort *605-255-4541*
Custer, SD 57730
www.custerstatepark.info

RUSHMORE MOUNTAIN SPORTS

Open year-round. Shuttles available for large groups.
505 North Main Street, Spearfish, SD 57783; 605-642-2885

SPEARFISH CANYON LODGE

P.O. Box 705, Spearfish, SD 57783; 605-584-3435 or 877-YRLODGE
www.spfcanyon.com

TWO WHEELER DEALER (two locations)

100 E. Blvd. N, Rapid City, SD 57701; 605-343-0524
215 E. Jackson, Spearfish, SD 57783; 605-642-7545
www.twowheelerdealer.com

HIGH COUNTRY GUEST RANCH & TRAIL RIDES

Open year-round.
12172 Deerfield Road (4 miles west of Hill City), Hill City, SD 57745;
605-574-9003
www.highcountryranch.com

TRAIL RIDES

Saddle up at one of these trail ride locations and explore the rustic Black Hills the traditional way—on horseback. Tour packages range from one hour to all-day rides.

ROCKIN R RIDES, INC. (two locations)

Allen Ranch

One-hour, half-day and overnight rides are offered. Tepees are available for rent at the Allen Ranch campground; wagon rides and cowboy cookouts can be arranged for large groups.

Hwy. 385 (east of Hot Springs), Hot Springs, SD 57747; 605-745-7868

Heritage Village

Hourly and half-day rides are available with a unique view of Crazy Horse Memorial.

(Hwy. 385 three miles north of Custer), Custer, SD 57730; 605-673-2999
Memorial Day through early September
www.rockingrtrailrides.com

HOLY SMOKE STABLES

One- and two-hour rides are offered through the Black Hills National Forest with views of Mount Rushmore.

Open mid-May through Labor Day.
24105 Hwy. 16A (1 mile north of Keystone), Keystone, SD 57751;
605-666-4444

KEYSTONE STABLES

Open May through September.
Hwy. 16A (1½ miles north of Keystone), Keystone, SD 57751; 605-666-4505

PALMER GULCH STABLES

One-hour to all-day trail rides are offered, along with cowboy breakfast rides and chuckwagon dinner rides on Tuesday and Thursday evenings, offering delicious western food and live cowboy entertainment.

Rides available Memorial Day through Labor Day.
Between Keystone and Hill City on Hwy. 244; 605-574-2525 ext. 812

BLUE BELL STABLES

One- and two-hour rides are available within Custer State Park.

Open Memorial Day to mid-September.
Blue Bell Lodge, Custer State Park; 605-255-4571

PARADISE VALLEY TRAIL RIDES

Open Memorial Day to Labor Day; Reservations requested.
Boxelder Forks Road, Nemo, SD 57759; 605-578-1249
www.paradisevalleyadventures.com

HIGH COUNTRY GUEST RANCH & TRAIL RIDES

This full-service resort offers hourly and half-day rides—as well as cabins for rent, an outdoor pool and mountain bike rentals. ATV rentals can also be arranged on-site. A cowboy breakfast is served for guests every morning. A cowboy supper, complete with horse-drawn wagon rides and cowboy poetry, is offered 2–3 nights per week in the summer for guests and the general public.

Open year-round.
12172 Deerfield Road (4 miles west of Hill City), Hill City, SD 57745;
605-574-9003
www.highcountryranch.com

ATV RENTALS

Nearly 5,000 miles of primitive roads criss-cross the Black Hills National Forest, offering perfect paths for all-terrain vehicles. Though the National Forest does not have a designated ATV trail system, riders are encouraged to follow the two-track dirt paths. Some of the off-limits areas include Spearfish Canyon, Black Elk Wilderness, the Mickelson Trail, campgrounds and lake areas. Other areas where you should not ride will be posted or gated. The U.S. Forest Service offers complimentary maps showing where ATV travel is permitted. Pick them up at a Forest Service office or visit www.fs.fed.us/r2/blackhills.

THUNDERHEAD RENTALS

Hwy. 14A, Lead, SD 57754; 605-584-2774

CUSTER CROSSING CAMPGROUND

Rentals available May through October. Rustic cabins and RV hook-ups on-site.
HCR 73 Box 1525 (15 miles south of Deadwood on Hwy. 385),
Deadwood, SD 57732; 605-584-1009

RECREATIONAL SPRINGS RESORT

Available May through early October. Lodging and restaurant available on-site.
12201 Hwy. 14A (8 miles south of Deadwood on Hwy. 85), Lead, SD 57754;
877-584-1228 or 605-584-3435
www.recsprings.com

DEERFIELD LAKE RESORT

Located along the Mickelson Trail for great hiking, biking and trail riding, this full-service resort boasts great trout fishing and rents cabins, canoes and offers horse boarding in addition to the ATV rentals. Snowmobiles can be rented in winter.

Open year-round.
11321 Gillette Prairie Road, Hill City, SD 57745; 605-574-2636
www.blackhills.com/mountainmeadow

MAD MOUNTAIN ADVENTURES

Open May through October.
21443 Hwy. 385 (6 miles south of Deadwood), Deadwood, SD 57732;
605-578-1878
www.madmountainadventures.com

Neat to Know: Winter Delights

➤ With its annual abundant snowfall, the Black Hills is transformed into an ideal winter getaway—offering two ski resorts, 350 miles of groomed snowmobile trails, cross-country skiing and even ice fishing.

DOWNHILL SKIING

DEER MOUNTAIN SKI AREA

In addition to downhill runs for skiing and snowboarding, this resort offers night skiing on Fridays and Saturdays and a snow-tubing area with a convenient tow-rope to pull you to the top of the hill. Rentals and lessons available.

Deer Mountain offers great hills for snowboarding as well as skiing and tubing.

3 miles South on Hwy. 385, Lead, SD 57754; 888-410-DEER
www.skideermountain.com

TERRY PEAK SKI AREA

Terry Peak offers five high-speed chairlifts and over 20 miles of groomed trails. Rentals and lessons available.

P.O. Box 774, Lead, SD 57754; 800-456-0524 or 605-584-2165
www.terrypeak.com

SNOWMOBILING

RECREATIONAL SPRINGS RESORT

12201 Hwy. 14A (8 miles south of Deadwood on Hwy. 85), Lead, SD 57754;
877-584-1228 or 605-584-1228
www.recsprings.com

SPEARFISH CANYON LODGE

Hwy. 14A Spearfish Canyon, Spearfish, SD 57783;
605-584-2207 or 800-439-8544 or 877-YRLODGE
www.spfcanyon.com

Snowmobiling in the Black Hills is a popular way to view the winter scenery. For trail conditions call the South Dakota Snowmobile Hotline at 800-445-3474.

PRESIDENTS PARK

11249 Presidents Park Loop, Lead, SD 57754; 605-584-9925
www.presidentspark.com

DEERFIELD LAKE RESORT

11321 Gillette Prairie Road, Hill City, SD 57745; 605-574-2636
www.blackhills.com/mountainmeadow

THUNDERHEAD RENTALS

Hwy. 14A, Lead, SD 57754; 605-584-2774

MAD MOUNTAIN ADVENTURES

21443 Hwy. 385 (6 milies south of Deadwood), Deadwood, SD 57732;
605-578-1878
www.madmountainadventures.com

ICE SKATING

ROOSEVELT PARK ICE ARENA

Offered year-round.
235 Waterloo Street, Rapid City, SD 57701; 605-394-6161

CHAPTER SEVEN

Water Parks, Go-Carts and Other Good Times

Create fun family memories at modern day adventures like a water park, mini-golf course, or go-cart track. Or, spend a leisurely afternoon at Storybook Island, one of the Black Hills' premier parks. And, for the ride of a lifetime, you can climb aboard an old-time steam train, a helicopter or even a hot air balloon.

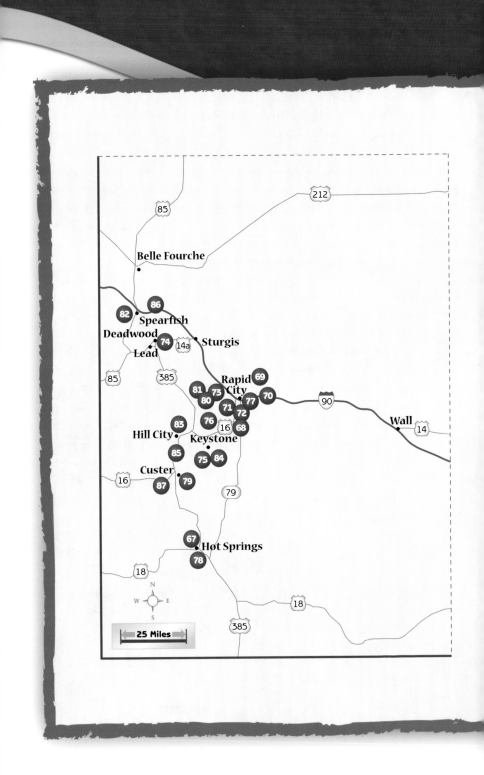

Wonderful Water Parks

Great Go-Carts and Amusement Parks

Magnificent Mini Golf

Perfect Parks

Thrill Rides

EVANS PLUNGE

Evans Plunge—the world's largest natural warm water indoor swimming pool—entertains all ages with its three water slides, fun-tubes, Tarzan rings and two kiddie pools with their own frog-themed slide.

At Hot Springs, take the plunge in thermal mineral water that's 87°!

The facility stands where it was originally founded in 1890, built over a group of small springs and one giant thermal spout of warm mineral water that keeps the pool a steady 87 degrees Fahrenheit. The springs flow up through the pebble bottom of the pool at a rate of 5,000 gallons per minute, ensuring fresh clean water at all times. The facility includes an outdoor pool open during the summer months.

Open year-round; Admission charged.
45 North River Street (on the north side of Hot Springs off Hwy. 385),
Hot Springs, SD 57747; 605-745-5165
www.evansplunge.com

Neat to Know: Hot Springs History

➤ Originally called Minnekahta, which means warm waters, the town's name was changed to Hot Springs in 1886. The large, rose-colored sandstone buildings that still line Hot Springs' charming streets were built in the late 19th century as elaborate hotels to pamper the throngs of people who came to play and be healed by the therapeutic, warm spring waters of the town. The mineral water contains calcium, potassium, lithium, magnesium, manganese and naturally occurring hydrogen peroxide, which pioneers believed to be useful in the treatment of chronic diseases and in relieving arthritis. Today, the sandstone structures, built from the rock of the surrounding ridges, have been renovated to include antique shops, restaurants, hotels, museums and—true to the town's history—bath houses and spa services.

➤ The **Springs Bath House** (605-745-4424 or www.springs-bathhouse.com) has been reconstructed on the site of the Sulfur Bath House that operated over a century ago. This modernized spa uses the same hot mineral spring as the original bath house to fill their outdoor soaking pool. Services offered include water therapies, as well as traditional full body massages and body wraps. Open daily through the summer and by appointment from November to April.

RUSHMORE WATERSLIDE

Nine exciting slides will help you keep your cool during a hot summer day. The waterpark area includes picnic grounds and unlimited mini-golf with admission.

Open June through mid-August; Admission charged.
1715 Catron Blvd., Rapid City, SD 57701; 605-348-8962
www.rushmorewaterslide.com

INDOOR WATERPARK AT BEST WESTERN RAMKOTA HOTEL

What a waterpark! This indoor theme-pool is surrounded by palm trees, a pirate ship, several kid-friendly slides and not one, but *two*, 165-foot water flume slides. The Ramkota is also home to **Minerva's**, one of the area's best restaurants, and is conveniently located next to the **Rushmore Mall**, making this a great getaway any time of year.

Open year-round; Complimentary for registered hotel guests.
2111 North LaCrosse Street (I-90 at Exit 59), Rapid City, SD 57701;
605-343-8550 or 800-528-1234
www.rapidcity.ramkota.com

WATIKI INDOOR WATERPARK RESORT

This is South Dakota's largest indoor waterpark. The 30,000-square-foot facility includes waterslides, a lazy float river, arcade, lounge and concession area all under one roof and adjacent to the La Quinta and Fairfield Inn & Suites.

Open year-round; Day passes available for a fee.
1416 North Elk Vale Rd (I-90 at Exit 61), Rapid City, SD 57701; 866-928-4543
www.watikiwaterpark.com

Neat to Know

➤ In Rapid City, **Jimmy Hilton Municipal Pool** (940 Sheridan Lake Road; 605-394-1894) at Sioux Park near Storybook Island, is no ordinary pool. It includes a family leisure pool, water slides and even a dinosaur. Open June to mid-August.

➤ The **Rapid City Swim Center** (235 Waterloo Street; 605-394-5223) offers indoor swimming year-round with two fun slides.

Great Go-Carts & Amusement Parks

THE RANCH AMUSEMENT PARK

There's something for everyone here. Activities include a ¾-mile go-cart track, a slick track for adults and kiddie karts for ages 5 and up. There's also a rock climbing wall, bumper cars, water bumper boats, two 18-hole mini-golf courses set in a Wild West theme, the Kiddy Bee ride, a snack bar and ice cream stand.

Open Memorial Day to Labor Day; Admission charged.
6303 S. Highway 16 (3 miles south of Rapid City on Hwy. 16),
Rapid City, SD 57701; 605-342-3321
www.ranchamusementpark.com

BLACK HILLS MAZE FAMILY ADVENTURE PARK

The main attraction at this family-friendly park is a 1⅛-mile labyrinth of walkways, bridges, stairs and towers to navigate through. Additional entertainment includes bankshot basketball, batting cages, water balloon wars, a 25-foot climbing wall and racing ziplines that swing over the top of the maze. A train ride is offered around the park for youngsters.

Open Memorial Day to Labor Day and weekends only in May and September;
Admission charged.
P.O. Box 1509 (3 miles south of Rapid City on Hwy. 16),
Rapid City, SD 57709; 605-343-5439
www.blackhillsmaze.com

FLAGS AND WHEELS INDOOR RACING

High energy entertainment is the name of the game at this indoor adventure park. Activities include go-carts, paintball, laser tag, bumper cars and batting cages.

Open daily through the summer and evenings and weekends
September through May; Admission charged.
405 12th Street (take Omaha Street to 12th Street),
Rapid City, SD 57701; 605-341-2186
www.flagsandwheels.com

GULCHES OF FUN AMUSEMENT PARK

Kids and adults will enjoy this fun park complete with go-carts, 18-hole mini-golf, bumper boats, a kiddie playland and game arcade.

Open Memorial Day through Labor Day; Admission charged.
225 Cliff Street, South Hwy. 85 (adjacent to the Comfort Inn),
Deadwood, SD 57732; 605-578-7550 or 800-961-3096
www.gulchesoffun.com

Magnificent Mini Golf

HOLY TERROR MINI GOLF

Designed with a gold mine theme, this 18-hole course is set against a steep mountain and includes putting around a waterwheel, millpond and mining sluices.

Open May 15 through October 31; Fee charged.
609 Hwy. 16A (next to the National Presidential Wax Museum),
Keystone, SD 57751; 605-666-4455
www.presidentialwaxmuseum.com/holyterrorgolf.asp

PUTZ-N-GLO

This indoor, Rock-n-Roll themed mini-golf course puts a new spin on the game with a black light and rock tunes from the last five decades. Snack bar and video arcade also on-site.

Open daily May through Labor Day; Limited hours October through April;
Fee charged.
23694 Strato Rim Road (2 miles past Bear Country on Hwy. 16),
Rapid City, SD 57702; 605-716-1230
www.putznglo.com

PIRATE'S COVE

Try a challenging round of mini golf at this 18-hole course, landscaped around a pirate theme, complete with caves, waterfalls and an abandoned ship.

Open Memorial Day through mid-October; Fee charged.
1500 LaCrosse Street, Rapid City, SD 57701; 605-343-8540
www.piratescove.net

PUTT-4-FUN

Find fun for the whole family at this 18-hole course set amid waterfalls, footbridges and sandtraps.

Open April to October, Fee charged.
640 South 6th Street (next to the Budget Host Hills Inn),
Hot Springs, SD 57747; 605-745-7888
www.putt4fun.us

GRIZZLY GULCH ADVENTURE GOLF

This is a rustic-themed course with plenty of obstacles to putt through, over and around.

Open May through early October.
W. Hwy. 16, Custer, SD 57730; 605-673-1021

Neat to Know

➤ For a premier golf experience in the shadow of Devils Tower, book a tee time at **Devils Tower Golf** (307-467-5773 or www.devilstowergolf.com) located on a bluff above historical Hulett, Wyoming. The course provides a scenic view of the Belle Fourche River Valley with Devils Tower looming on the horizon. Consisting of 650 acres, the course currently offers 9 holes, but will eventually encompass 18 holes of championship golf.

Perfect Parks

STORYBOOK ISLAND

A fantasy of castles and nursery rhyme characters greet children in this popular outdoor park. Dr. Suess, Winnie the Pooh, Cinderella and over 100 other fairy tale characters are on display among shady picnic areas and playground equipment. The tiny children's train is a favorite for all youngsters, as is the McDonald's Free Children's Theater, which performs 30-minute musical dramas several times daily throughout the summer.

Noah's Ark is just one of the adorable stories come to life at Rapid City's Storybook Island.

Open Memorial Day through Labor Day; Free admission.
1301 Sheridan Lake Road, P.O. Box 9196, Rapid City, SD 57709; 605-342-6357
www.storybookisland.org

Neat to Know

➤ In December, Storybook Island is bedecked in Christmas lights for a walk-through wonderland. Santa greets children of all ages in the gift shop.

CANYON LAKE PARK

Located on the west side of Rapid City, this family-friendly setting allows visitors to feed the ducks and geese, rent a paddle boat, stroll over the bridge to the gazebo on the island or try their luck fishing. Numerous picnic and playground areas surround the area.

Nearby, the Lake Park Campground (2850 Chapel Lane, 800-644-2267 or 605-341-5320) rents furnished cottages and camping sites.

Accessible year-round.
4181 Jackson Boulevard, Rapid City, SD 57701; 605-394-4175

SPEARFISH CITY PARK

Located along Spearfish Creek (and adjacent to the D.C. Booth Historic Fish Hatchery, see Chapter 2, page 30), this shady park is a picturesque place to enjoy the outdoors. Feeding the fish at the hatchery is a favorite activity for young and old visitors. A paved path for biking or walking winds along the creek and meanders through the town. A large, castle-like playground at the park will entertain kids for hours. On hot days, consider bringing your own inner tube to float along the shallow creek's cool waters. Fishing on the creek is also popular. Spearfish City Campground is within walking distance (605-642-1340). Bicycles can be rented at Rushmore Mountain Sports, 505 North Main Street, Spearfish (605-642-2885).

Accessible year-round.
Canyon Street, Spearfish, SD 57783; 605-642-1333

FOR MORE PARKS, SEE ALSO

Chapter 3: Dinosaur Park, Rapid City, page 40; Flintstones Bedrock City, Custer, page 40

Thrill Rides

For a one-of-a-kind way to view the beauty of the Black Hills, consider taking a train, plane, helicopter or hot air balloon ride. Whichever you choose, be prepared for the experience of a lifetime.

1880 TRAIN—BLACK HILLS CENTRAL RAILROAD

Hop aboard the 1880 Train at Hill City or Keystone to enjoy the scenery of the Black Hills from a vintage steam train—one of America's last steam trains still in service. The twenty-mile, two-hour round trip follows the original route of the CB&Q Railroad line, which was laid down in the late 1880s to service the mines and mills between Hill City and Keystone. En route you'll see vistas of the Black Hills National Forest and Harney Peak, South Dakota's tallest mountain. Reservations are recommended. Depots in both Hill City and Keystone feature gift shops with train memorabilia.

Ride the rails on the Black Hills Central Railroad that runs between Hill City and Keystone.

May through early October; Admission charged.
P.O. Box 1880, Hill City, SD 57745; 605-574-2222
www.1880Train.com

Neat to Know

➤ While in Hill City to catch the 1880 Train, make a point to eat lunch or dinner at the well-known **Alpine Inn** (605-574-2749). The restaurant is housed in the former Harney Peak Hotel building, which was built in 1886 and is a charming, historical landmark on Hill City's Main Street. The decor and lunch menu with a European flair were influenced by the German mother-daughter duo who opened the restaurant in 1984 and still operate it today. The popular dinner, served 5–10 pm, features just one entrée: filet mignon, a lettuce wedge, baked potato and Texas toast. And save room for dessert— over 30 delightful choices are offered. Open year-round; Closed Sundays.

RUSHMORE TRAMWAY AND PRESIDENT'S ALPINE SLIDE

Offering scenic views of Mount Rushmore, your adventure begins with a chairlift ride up the mountain. At the summit, you can grab a bobsled and ride down the thrilling 2,000 feet of track filled with dips, twists and turns. Riders can control their own speed, but for those not willing to ride the slide, the tramway will return riders to the base of the hill. Also atop the mountain are walkways to enjoy the view and a restaurant serving burgers and ice cream.

Open Memorial Day to Labor Day; Admission charged.
Hwy. 16A, P.O. Box 112, Keystone, SD 57751; 605-666-4478
www.presidentsslide.com

BLACK HILLS AERIAL ADVENTURES

A variety of helicopter tour packages are offered for high-altitude views of the Black Hills and its monuments.

Open mid-May through mid-September; Fee charged.
Hwy. 385 (2 miles north of Crazy Horse), Custer, SD 57730; 605-673-2163

EAGLES' VIEW AIR TOURS

Enjoy the Black Hills scenery and monuments with a personal airplane tour. Package options include a 30-minute Spearfish Canyon tour, 70-minute Devils Tower tour, 80-minute Mount Rushmore tour, or 2-hour "see it all" tour that includes Spearfish Canyon, Devils Tower, Mount Rushmore, Crazy Horse and Deadwood.

Tours offered year round; Fee charged.
300 Aviation Place, Spearfish, SD 57783; 605-642-4112 or 800-843-8010
www.eagleaviationinc.com

BLACK HILLS BALLOONS

Floating high above the earth in a hot air balloon, you'll see spectacular scenes of Mount Rushmore, Crazy Horse, scenic lakes and herds of wildlife. The balloon pilots are federally licensed and can carry 2 to 12 passengers per balloon. Flights take approximately two to three hours and are offered at sunrise. Advance reservations required.

See the Black Hills area from a bird's eye view in a hot air balloon.

Offered weather permitting; Fee charged.
P.O. Box 210, Custer, SD 57730; 605-673-2520 or 800-568-5320
www.rapidnet.com/~balloons/

FOR OTHER FUN RIDES, SEE ALSO:

Chapter 2: Buffalo Safari Jeep Rides, State Game Lodge and Resort, Custer State Park, page 29

Chapter 6: bicycle rentals, page 87; trail rides, page 88; ATV rentals, page 89; snowmobile rentals, page 91

Chapter 9: hayrides and chuckwagon cookouts, Blue Bell Lodge, Custer State Park, page 120–122

CHAPTER EIGHT

Histories and Oddities

No vacation would be complete without unexpected detours to marvel at one-of-a-kind roadside attractions. And the Black Hills offer an array of unique destinations—from historical sites to bewildering wonders. Take time to visit some of these uncommon places and you may be surprised to find that it becomes the highlight of your trip.

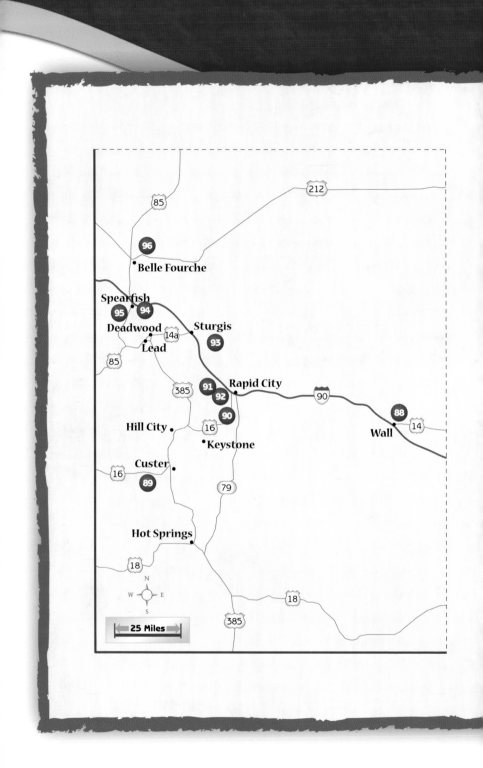

Roadside Wonders

WALL DRUG

Once a simple, small-town drugstore in the 1930s, Wall Drug has grown to a shopping emporium complete with a western art gallery and clothing store, a bookstore stocked with a varied selection by regional authors, a fudge shop, rock shop, jewelry store and kitschy items to fit every tourist's fancy—including jackalopes, turd birds, T-shirts and even a selection of red hats for the ladies of the Red Hat Society.

Ted Hustead established Wall Drug in the 1930s. Today it's a shopping emporium, consuming most of Wall's Main Street.

Established in 1909, Wall Drug was just another pharmacy until it was purchased by Ted Hustead and his wife Dorothy in 1931. After five years of dismal business during the Great Depression, Dorothy had a brain-storm to put signs and billboards along the highway, offering free ice water at Wall Drug. The promotion attracted several weary travelers and shortly thereafter, Wall Drug was no longer just a pharmacy. The western store, restaurant and souvenir merchandise were soon added to their now-famous offer of free ice water.

In the decades since, Wall Drug billboards can still be found around the globe (and many continue to promote free ice water). Today, the third generation of the Hustead family operates the gussied-up drugstore on Wall's Main Street. Open year-round, it still houses a pharmacy, but mainly caters to tourists—with as many as 20,000 visitors a day stopping at Wall Drug during the peak summer season.

The restaurant still features homemade donuts and five-cent coffee. If you're there for dinner, try the buffalo burger and a slice of homemade pie.

Be sure to take a gander at the silver dollar collection in the restaurant's countertop, with dates ranging from 1878 to 1928.

Other don't-miss attractions include one of the best western art galleries in the region, several historical photographs, original paintings and sculptures—some by Mount Rushmore sculptor Gutzon Borglum and South Dakota native Harvey Dunn.

Wall Drug billboards are a familiar sight on a trip to the Black Hills.

Amid the shopping is memorabilia, a wooden cowboy, Indian figures and even a Travelers Chapel for a quiet moment of reflection. Wall Drug's Back Yard is geared for children with a roaring T-Rex, a 6-foot rabbit, a buckin' horse to climb on and, of course, the famous free ice water. Kids can also tour a replica of a gold mine and pan for their very own gems.

Open year round; Free admission.
510 Main Street, P.O. Box 401, Wall, SD 57790; 605-279-2175
www.walldrug.com

FOUR MILE OLD WEST TOWN

Narrated hayrides or self-guided walking tours through this historical "ghost town" feature the buildings, furnishings and artifacts of the nineteenth century. The Wild West Show is performed at 6 pm on Thursday and Friday, from Memorial Day through Labor Day.

Open May through October; Admission charged.
RR1 Box 57E, Hwy. 16 West (4 miles west of Custer), Custer, SD 57730;
605-673-3905
www.fourmilesd.com

Neat to Know: Towns of Yesteryear

➤ The **1880 Town** (605-344-2259; www.1880town.com), located 150 miles east of Rapid City on I-90 at Exit 170, was intended to be a movie set and re-creates an Old West prairie town. Buildings include a jail, saloon, barbershop, log cabin, church and schoolhouse. Snacks are available on-site. Open May through October; Admission charged.

➤ An example of the classic general store from a century ago can be found in the **Aladdin General Store** (307-896-2226; www.aladdinwy.com), which is complete with roll-top flour bins and original counters. Now listed on the National Register of Historic Places, the store offers books, clothing, antiques and art. Two miles east of the store is a restored "tipple," a structure used to load coal directly from a mine into railroad cars. Located west of Belle Fourche on Hwy. 34 on the way to Devils Tower or 9 miles north of I-90 at Exit 199. Open year-round.

➤ **Rockerville**—9 miles south of Rapid City on Hwy. 16 and on the way to Mount Rushmore—was a thriving community during the Gold Rush Days of the 1880s. Today, the store-fronts are all boarded up, leaving a perfectly preserved ghost town (with the exception of the bustling **Gas Light Restaurant and Saloon** (605-343-9276), which serves steaks, seafood and pasta.

COSMOS MYSTERY AREA

Science and the laws of nature seem to be defied at this "mystery area," as a ball rolls uphill and other demonstrations show people standing on the wall or at an angle, despite being on level ground. It's one of those places you just have to see to believe.

Open April through October; Admission charged.
3616 West Main (17 miles south of Rapid City along Hwy. 16), Rapid City, SD 57702; 605-343-9802
www.cosmosmysteryarea.com

Cosmos Mystery Area offers unique family fun by defying gravity.

CHAPEL IN THE HILLS

Adorned with intricate woodcarvings, this church is a replica of the 850-year-old Stavkirke (Stave Church) in Norway. Surrounded by a serene park setting, the church is a popular place for summer weddings. There's also a Norwegian Log Cabin Museum and a grass-roofed log building that houses a gift shop. Vespers are held nightly at the church at 7:30 pm from the second Sunday in June through the last Sunday in August.

Intricate woodcarvings make this replica Stavkirke an interesting place to visit in Rapid City.

Open May to October; Free admission.
3788 Chapel Lane (Hwy. 44 West), Rapid City, SD 57702; 605-342-8281

BERLIN WALL EXHIBIT IN MEMORIAL PARK

Near Rapid Creek and the Rushmore Civic Center, this outdoor exhibit features two 12-foot segments of the Berlin Wall, accompanied by photos and informational displays. A rose garden and memorials to pioneers, veterans and victims of Rapid's 1972 flood are also part of the park.

Open year-round; Free admission.
444 Mt. Rushmore Road, P.O. Box 9331, Rapid City, SD 57709; 605-343-1744
www.rcgov.org/parks_recreation/parks/berlin_wall_exhibit.htm

PETRIFIED FOREST OF THE BLACK HILLS

The geology of the Black Hills is showcased with an interpretive film about the region's rocks and minerals, as well as 25 acres of petrified forest to explore. The area includes the Gallery of Stone Rock Shop and is adjacent to a large RV park with camping, cabins and a heated pool.

Open Memorial Day through September; Admission charged.
8228 Elk Creek Road, I-90 Exit 46, Piedmont, SD 57769;
605-787-4884 or 800-846-2267
www.elkcreek.org

Neat to Know

➤ One hundred miles east of Rapid City, the **Badlands Petrified Gardens** at Kadoka, South Dakota (605-837-2448, I-90 Exit 152) includes a large display of petrified trees and prehistoric fossils. Open mid-April through October; Admission charged.

TERMESPHERE GALLERY

Art enthusiasts will marvel at the Termesphere Gallery featuring the work of artist Dick Termes, who paints on spheres. Nearly 30 "termespheres" rotate from ceiling motors in his sphere-shaped home gallery outside Spearfish. Termespheres can also be viewed at the Adams Museum in Deadwood (see page 56) and the Spearfish City Library.

Call for gallery hours;
Free admission.
1920 Christensen Drive,
Spearfish, SD 57783; 605-642-4805
www.termespheres.com

"Brain Strain" is just one of nearly 30 termespheres on display in Spearfish.

Neat to Know

➤ In the heart of Spearfish is the quaint campus of **Black Hills State University**. Founded in 1883, it was the first college built in South Dakota and was originally named Dakota Normal School.

THOEN STONE MONUMENT

Though General Custer and his expedition are credited with finding gold in the Black Hills in 1874, it is believed the Ezra Kind party was truly the first to discover gold in the Black Hills in 1834—forty years earlier. However, the seven men in the party were killed by Indians before they could return home. But, before his death, Kind etched their story on a stone, which was discovered at the base of Spearfish's Lookout

Mountain in 1887 by Louis Thoen. The original stone, named in Thoen's honor, is on display in the Adams Museum in Deadwood (see page 56). To view the marker denoting the original location of the stone, go through the Passion Play amphitheater parking lot and follow the path up the hill. For more information contact the Spearfish Chamber of Commerce (605-642-2626).

Spearfish, SD

GEOGRAPHIC CENTER OF THE UNITED STATES

In 1959, Belle Fourche was given special acclaim as the "Center of the Nation" by the U.S. Coast and Geodetic Survey, after Alaska and Hawaii were admitted to the Union that same year. Formerly, when only America's 48 states were considered, the center of the nation was deemed to be at Smith Center, Kansas. A plaque noting Belle's special designation is on display outside the Belle Fourche Chamber's Visitor Information Center (605-892-2676), adjacent to the Tri-State Memorial Museum. To reach the actual marker, which is 20 miles north of Belle Fourche, at latitude 63 degrees 50'N and longitude 152 degrees 00'W, follow U.S. 85 north from Belle Fourche 13 miles. Turn west on Harding Road, also known as Old Highway 85, and drive 7⅗ miles.

Belle Fourche, SD

Neat to Know

> ➤ Bentonite, which is mined near Belle Fourche, can be found in everyday products such as crayons, glue, paint, shoe polish and spark plugs.

CHAPTER NINE

Puttin' On A Show

Entertainment abounds in the Black Hills, and much of it is set to music. From Old West settings to Broadway-style shows, there's something for every taste. So kick up your heels and treat the family to a night out and a special show. Your outing just might become a family tradition each time you visit the Black Hills.

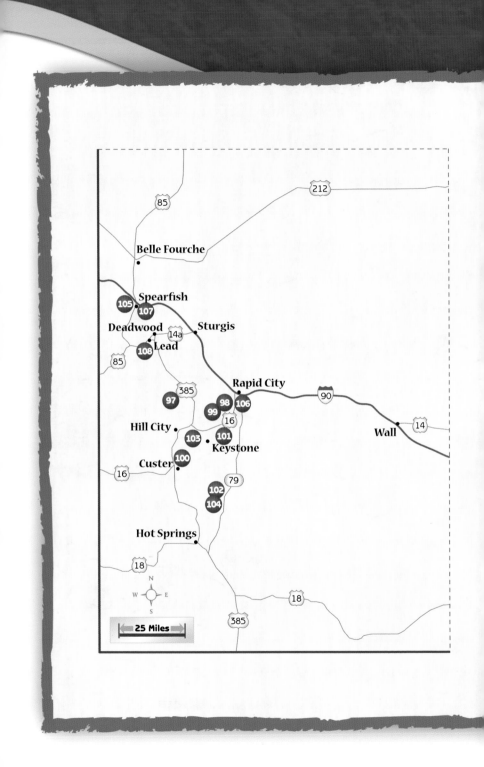

Western Style

Summer Sensations

Year-round Curtain Calls

If it's a chuckwagon dinner and western music show you hunger for, there are several options during the summer throughout the Hills.

CIRCLE B RANCH CHUCKWAGON SUPPER AND WESTERN MUSIC SHOW

Set amid the forest of the Black Hills, the Circle B Ranch includes the store fronts of a western town, mini-golf, gold panning, an on-site wood carver, a children's playground and wagon trail and pony rides. The ranch opens at 5 pm daily and the dinner bell rings at 6:30 pm. Dinner is served cowboy-style on a tin plate and is followed by an entertaining music show.

Open Memorial Day through mid-September, limited schedule after Labor Day; Fee charged.
22735 Hwy. 385 (12 miles west of Rapid City), Rapid City, SD 57702;
605-348-7358 or 800-403-7358
www.circle-b-ranch.com

FORT HAYS CHUCKWAGON SUPPER AND SHOW

This traditional cowboy supper and musical begins at 6:30 pm. Along with dinner, visitors can view the movie set from *Dances With Wolves*, which was filmed in South Dakota, and browse the western gift shops.

Additionally, the Fort Hays Chuckwagon serves all-you-can eat cowboy pancakes each morning until 11 am. And, if you like, you can book a day-long chartered bus tour of the Black Hills that starts at Fort Hays with the breakfast and ends with the chuckwagon show.

Open mid-May thru early October; Fee charged.
8181 Mount Rushmore Road (4 miles south of Rapid City on Hwy16),
P.O. Box 264,
Rapid City, SD 57709;
605-394-9653 or
888-394-9653
http://www.blackhillsattractions.com/pages/attractions/fthays.html

Entertainment is part of the menu at a Black Hills Chuckwagon Show.

FLYING T CHUCKWAGON SUPPER AND SHOW

Western music and a slice of comedy are served up with dinner nightly at 6:30 pm. The show runs from 7–8 pm.

Open mid-May through Labor Day, limited schedule in September; Fee charged.
8971 South Hwy. 16 (6 miles south of Rapid City next to Reptile Gardens),
Rapid City, SD 57702; 605-342-1905 or 888-256-1905
www.flyingt.com

HERITAGE VILLAGE

Experience the West in this fun-filled village that offers an Old West town for kids, a rodeo clown museum and a western music show at 7:45 pm nightly (except Monday), featuring songs like "Tumblin' Tumbleweeds," "Cool Water" and "Ghost Riders in the Sky." After the program, watch the Laser Light Show at Crazy Horse just down the road. The village includes several gift shops, a restaurant serving breakfast, lunch and dinner buffets and an adjacent campground with trail rides.

Open May through early October, limited performance schedule
after Labor Day; Fee charged.
1 Village Ave. (1 mile from Crazy Horse Memorial), Custer, SD 57730;
605-673-4761 or 888-428-3386
www.heritage-village.com

SOUTH DAKOTA'S PITCHFORK FONDUE AND DINNER SHOW

Guests get a cowboy hat and bandana to get them in the cowboy spirit at this special show where steaks are skewered on a pitchfork for barbecuing. The show, featuring Americana music, is part of a fun-filled dining experience and ends in time for you to enjoy the 9 pm Evening Lighting Ceremony at Mount Rushmore. Dinner seating begins at 5:30 pm. Located behind the Rushmore Borglum Center.

Open Memorial Day through mid-September; Fee charged.
610 Hwy. 16A, P.O. Box 664, Keystone, SD 57751;
605-666-4466 or 800-667-9870
www.rushmoreviewinn.com/pitchfork_fondue.htm

Neat to Know

➤ The **Comedy Western Gunfight** is presented three times daily on Keystone's Main Street at the Red Garter Saloon (605-666-4274). The rustic cowboy actors look tough, but it's just an act—this is a family show. Presented Memorial Day through Labor Day; Admission charged.

BLUE BELL LODGE HAYRIDE AND CHUCKWAGON COOKOUT

You'll hop aboard a hayride for this evening outing. Guests are treated to a souvenir hat and bandana and serenaded with cowboy songs as the old-time wagon makes its way to a meadow in Custer State Park for a steak fry. Hayrides depart at 5 pm nightly from Blue Bell Lodge. For reservations call 605-255-4531 or 800-658-3530. (For more about Custer State Park, see pages 28 and 73.)

Cookout offered Memorial Day to early October; Fee charged.
Custer State Park; 605-255-4515
www.custerstatepark.info

CHUCKWAGON DINNER RIDE AT PALMER GULCH STABLES

Climb aboard this chuckwagon for a ride into the Black Hills National Forest with great food and campfire songs. Dinner rides offered Tuesday and Thursday evenings.

Available Memorial Day through Labor Day; Fee charged.
Between Keystone and Hill City on Hwy. 244; 605-574-2525 ext. 812

Summer Sensations

Broadway performances in the Black Hills? Yes, it's true. These venues garner great acclaim throughout the region.

BLACK HILLS PLAYHOUSE

In 1945, the first Black Hills Playhouse performance was given in the tranquility of Custer State Park and the live theater productions have thrilled audiences ever since. Six Broadway-quality shows are presented throughout the summer season in this one-of-a-kind setting in the park.

Performances presented Memorial Day through Labor Day; Admission charged.
Custer State Park; 605-255-4141 or 605-255-4551
www.blackhillsplayhouse.com

BLACK HILLS PASSION PLAY

Set in a picturesque outdoor amphitheater, a cast of over 150 people, along with camels, donkeys, horses and sheep, recreate the dramatic events of the last seven days in the life of Christ. For a historical background of the Passion Play, which first opened in Spearfish in 1939, consider taking the guided backstage tours that are offered every day, except Saturday, at 12:30 and 3:30 pm. You'll also get glimpses of costumes, props and animals in the show. The Passion Play runs every Tuesday, Thursday and Sunday during the summer at 8 pm.

June 1 through August 31; Admission charged.
P.O. Box 489, Spearfish, SD 57783; 605-642-2646 or 800-457-0160
www.blackhills.com/bhpp

Year-round Curtain Calls

Community theater productions are presented at the following locations throughout the year. Although most are intended for adult audiences, some offer special productions geared for children during their season. Call or check their websites for a list of upcoming performances.

BLACK HILLS COMMUNITY THEATRE

Five unique performances are offered during the annual season, which runs from September through May. Productions are presented in the 170-seat theater at the Dahl Arts Center, located at Seventh and Quincy near downtown Rapid City.

713 Seventh Street, Rapid City, SD 57701; 605-394-1786
www.bhct.org

MATTHEWS OPERA HOUSE THEATER

This 1906 opera house was completely restored in 1997 and features five professional productions throughout the year.

614 Main Street, Spearfish, SD 57783; 605-642-7973
www.moh-scah.com

HISTORIC HOMESTAKE OPERA HOUSE

Completed in August 1914, the Homestake Opera House was built with stunning craftsmanship and was soon known as the "Jewel of the Black Hills." In addition to providing a venue for quality theater, it housed a recreation building that included a bowling alley, pool hall and swimming pool. Having endured two major fires, today the Opera House is undergoing massive reconstruction to restore the interior and recreation building. Performances are held intermittently throughout the year, and tours are offered at 11 am and 3 pm, Monday through Friday, or by appointment. Donations are requested for the tours to help fund restoration efforts.

313 Main Street, Lead, SD 57754; 605-584-2067
www.leadoperahouse.org/

FOR OTHER ENTERTAINING PERFORMANCES, SEE ALSO:

Chapter 1: Evening Lighting Ceremony, Mt. Rushmore, Keystone, page 13; Gunslingers re-enactment and Trial of Jack McCall, Deadwood, page 20

Chapter 7: Storybook Island Children's Theatre, Rapid City, page 101

Chapter 8: Four Mile Old West Town Wild West Show, page 111

For your convenience, we have provided you with two separate indexes. The first is alphabetical and includes both cities and featured sites. The second is a city index with featured sites within each city.

Index

Index by City

You've found the right place to go for more information about the stuff featured in the cities in this book.

ALADDIN, WY

- Aladdin General Store 112

BELLE FOURCHE (www.bellefourche.org)

This northern Black Hills town was so named by settlers because it is located at a "beautiful fork" in the river.

- Geographic Center of the United States 115
- Orman Dam 83
- Tri-State Memorial Museum 59

BELVEDERE

- 1880 Town 112

CUSTER (www.custersd.com)

Founded in 1875 after gold was discovered in French Creek, Custer was the first city established in the Black Hills and was named after Lt. Colonel George Armstrong Custer.

- Black Hills Aerial Adventures 104
- Black Hills Balloons 105
- Black Hills Playhouse 75, 122
- Blue Bell Lodge and Resort 76
- Blue Bell Lodge Hayride and Chuckwagon Cookout 122
- Blue Bell Stables 88
- Buffalo Safari Jeep Rides 29
- Crazy Horse Memorial 17
- Custer County 1881 Courthouse Museum 60
- Custer State Park 28, 73, 87
- Flintstones Bedrock City 40
- Fort We-Like-It Campground 87
- Four Mile Old West Town 111
- Frontier Photo 61
- Grizzly Gulch Adventure Golf 100
- Heritage Village 121
- Harney Peak 73
- hiking trails 73
- Iron Mountain Road 77
- Jewel Cave National Monument 84
- Legion Lake Resort 76, 87
- National Museum of Woodcarving 50
- Peter Norbeck Visitor Center and Scenic Byway 73
- Rockin R Rides/Heritage Village 88
- State Game Lodge and Resort 76, 87

DEADWOOD/LEAD (www.deadwood.org and www.lead.sd.us)

Deadwood earned its name during the late 1876 Gold Rush days because of the dead timber lining the gulch of the surrounding area. Sister city Lead (pronounced LEED) was named for the lead (or lode) in the region that has been yielding gold for more than a century.

HILL CITY (www.hillcitysd.com)

Originally known as Hillyo in 1876, this was the second city founded in the Black Hills and was later called Hill City.

- 1880 Train—Black Hills Central Railroad 103
- Alpine Inn 104
- Deerfield Lake and Resort 83, 89, 91
- Everything Prehistoric and Black Hills Institute of Geological Research 39
- High Country Guest Ranch and Trail Rides 88, 89
- Looking Back Photo Co. 61
- Prairie Berry Winery 50
- Rabbit Bicycle 87
- Sheridan Lake 82
- Sylvan Rocks 78

HOT SPRINGS (www.hotsprings-sd.com)

This southern Black Hills town gets its name from the many natural warm springs in the area. Initially called Minnekahta (warm waters) by settlers in 1879, the town's name was changed to Hot Springs in 1886.

- Angostura Reservoir Recreation Area 83
- Black Hills Wild Horse Sanctuary 29
- Cascade Falls/Keith Park 30
- Evans Plunge 96
- Mammoth Site 36
- Pioneer Historical Museum 59
- Putt-4-Fun 100
- Rockin R Rides/Allen Ranch 88
- Springs Bath House 97
- Wind Cave National Park 85

HULETT, WY (www.hulett.org)

- Devils Tower Golf 100
- Devils Tower National Monument 78
- Keyhole State Park 83

KADOKA

- Badlands Petrified Gardens 114

KEYSTONE (www.keystonechamber.com)

Gold mining gave this town its name in 1891 when the Keystone Gold Mine was established.

- 1880 Train—Black Hills Central Railroad 103
- Beautiful Rushmore Cave 86
- Big Thunder Gold Mine 46
- Black Hills Glass Blowers 49
- Borglum Historical Center 57
- Buffalo Old Time Photo Co. 61

RAPID CITY (cont.)

- Flags and Wheels Indoor Racing 99
- Flying T Chuckwagon Supper and Show 121
- Fort Hays Chuckwagon Supper and Show 120
- Indoor Waterpark at Best Western Ramkota Hotel 97
- Jimmy Hilton Municipal Pool 98
- Journey Museum, The 56
- Landstrom's Black Hills Gold Creations 48
- Minerva's 97
- Mount Rushmore Black Hills Gold Factory and Outlet Store 48
- Museum of Geology 39
- Old MacDonald's Petting Farm 27
- Pactola Reservoir 82
- Pirate's Cove 100
- Putz-n-Glo 99
- Ranch Amusement Park, The 98
- Rapid City Swim Center 98
- Reptile Gardens 26
- Roosevelt Park Ice Arena 91
- Rushmore Mall 97
- Rushmore Waterslide 97
- Sioux Pottery 49
- Sitting Bull Crystal Caverns 86
- South Dakota Air and Space Museum, (Ellsworth Air Force Base) 64
- Stamper Black Hills Gold Jewelry 48
- Storybook Island 101
- Thunderhead Underground Falls 86
- Two Wheeler Dealer 87
- Watiki Indoor Waterpark Resort 98

ROCHFORD

- Rochford Riders 87

ROCKERVILLE

- Rockerville Ghost Town 112
- Gas Light Restaurant and Saloon 112

SPEARFISH (www.spearfish.sd.us)

Often dubbed the "Queen City" because three high hills—Crow Peak, Spearfish Mountain and Lookout Mountain—surround the city like a crown, this town got its name from the Indians who speared fish in the crystal clear waters of Spearfish Creek.

- Black Hills Passion Play 67, 122
- Black Hills State University 114
- Cheyenne Crossing 73
- D.C. Booth Historic National Fish Hatchery 30
- Dolls at Home Museum 67

- Eagles' View Air Tours 104
- High Plains Western Heritage Center 57
- Iron Creek Lake 83
- Matthews Opera House Theater 123
- Rushmore Mountain Sports 87
- Spearfish Canyon and Lodge 72, 87, 91
- Spearfish City Park and Campground 102
- Spirit of the Hills Wildlife Sanctuary 30
- Termesphere Gallery 114
- Thoen Stone Monument 114
- Two Wheeler Dealer 87
- Vore Buffalo Jump (3½ miles west of Beulah, WY) 63
- Wickiup Village 73

STURGIS (www.sturgis.sd.us)

Founded in 1878, Sturgis was named for Colonel Samuel Sturgis, a commander at the nearby Fort Meade Cavalry Post.

- Bear Butte State Park 79
- Black Hills National Cemetery 58
- Centennial Trail 80
- Fort Meade Museum 58
- Sturgis Motorcycle Museum and Hall of Fame 65

WALL (www.wall-badlands.com/home.asp)

Established as a railroad station in 1907, this town gets its name from the rugged "wall" of the Badlands that rises up from the prairie.

- Badlands National Park 37
- Legacy Old Time Photo 61
- Minuteman Missile National Historic Site (20 miles east of Wall) 64
- National Grasslands Visitor Center 67
- Prairie Homestead 38
- Wall Drug 38, 110
- Wildlife Museum 67
- Wild West Wax Museum 21
- Wounded Knee: The Museum 63

About the Author

Kindra Gordon first began spinning stories when she was in second grade and still enjoys the thrill of putting words on paper everyday. Raised on a ranch in South Dakota, she is an agricultural journalism graduate from South Dakota State University in Brookings. Today she works as a freelance writer for national cattle magazines, including *BEEF*, *Western Cowman*, and the *Angus Journal*. She has also written travel articles for AAA's *Home&Away* magazine and has taught newspaper design and feature writing as an adjunct professor in the Mass Communications Department at Black Hills State University in Spearfish, South Dakota.

Kindra and her husband Bruce live near Sturgis, South Dakota with their four young children, and they wake up everyday to an inspiring view of the Black Hills.

Contact Information:
Kindra Gordon
11734 Weisman Road
Whitewood, SD 57793
e-mail: office@gordonresources.com